"An exhilarating look at a woman's journey to find true love and happiness. An honest look at love in the 21st century...with all its twists and turns."

—Shannen McHale, Viewer Relations, The Tonight Show with Jay Leno

"*Singing the Song of Life* was a good reminder of how universal life's ups and downs are and how resilient some people can be even in the worst of circumstances."

— Lila Lazarus, Detroit TV personality

"Debra's memoirs made me examine and look inside myself, my mistakes, my emotionally based decisions and the consequences that they create.

I was particularly captivated by the honesty of this story. It's not easy to present a truly honest piece of work and put yourself out there. Although this is from a woman's point of view, all can benefit and relate to this. *Singing the Song of Life: One Woman's Symphony* is a must read. I would also suggest that you pass it along to your teenage children as it would serve as a story of courage, strength and perseverance."

—Anthony Gigante, Executive Producer-Cugini www.cuginithemovie.com

My Professional Konnection
Marilyn Kirschner/Public Relations
For Further Info Contact:
661-645-6741

"I couldn't put *Singing the Song of Life* down. Debra takes her readers on a fast journey of personal growth. It was amazing to watch a woman learn and grow from her mistakes while never giving up on her dreams. I was mesmerized by her story. Debra shows us how to celebrate life."

— Joyce Weiss, author of *Take the Ride of Your Life!* and group dynamics specialist

Debra Beryle's book *Singing the Song of Life* is like sitting down with your best friend and hearing her life's journey. The author tells her story with courage, applying humor and insight to life's toughest challenges. Beryle gives us all hope, that though life can take us to some pretty dark places; we can come out stronger, wiser and shining even brighter.

Compelling and fast paced.. I highly recommend this memoir."

— Dale Sparage, Fine Art Photographer/Educator, MFA BFA BA

"First, let me tell you that this book is not for the young ones. You read about it all in this book – adventure, friendship, marriage [and all the good things that come with it, which is why it's not really for the young ones], divorce – it's all wrapped up in this book! I really like that each chapter of the book [which falls in line with each chapter of her life] follows along the path of a song. One of my favorite things was at the beginning of each chapter, reading the song title for that chapter and trying to guess what was going to happen. It was quite an exciting book to read! From the highs, to the lows, back to the highs, it was fun."

— Kendahl Andrade, *Stepmom Extraordinaire*

"Dori feels real in this book because she is real and that's what really made this book for me. Dori is not a Hollywood starlet, she is an everyday woman, trying to succeed, trying to find love and trying to find peace with herself.

This is an amazing book. I was enthralled. It reads like a novel with never a dull moment, I was always wondering what will happen to Dori next, how she would handle it and hoping for something great for her. It's an inspiring book, because as tough as things got for Ms. Beryle, she never gave up, she kept pulling herself back up. She also does not place blame, which is refreshing. She knows she had some problems and works out where the problems came from but never plays the 'pitiful me' card. An absolutely inspiring and genuine read, I can't recommend this enough. Even if you don't read memoirs, you should read this one - it applies in some way to all of us. Each one of us has been there and can relate to something in Ms. Beryle's life and hopefully we can take away her strength and become stronger women ourselves. You may find yourself singing along, like I did with Ms. Beryle's symphony."

— Crystal Fulcher, *My Reading Room*

Love Life,
Debra Beryle

Singing The Song of Life

ONE WOMAN'S SYMPHONY

By

Debra Beryle

Langdon Street Press
212 3rd Avenue North, Suite 290
Minneapolis, MN 55401
612.455.2293
www.langdonstreetpress.com

www.SingingTheSongofLife.com

ISBN - 978-1-934938-51-5
ISBN - 1-934938-51-3
LCCN - 2009933759

Book sales for North America and international:
Itasca Books, 3501 Highway 100 South, Suite 220
Minneapolis, MN 55416
Phone: 952.345.4488 (toll free 1.800.901.3480)
Fax: 952.920.0541; email to orders@itascabooks.com

Printed in the United States of America

LANGDON
STREET PRESS

"Keep it in your heart that the ones you love are life's most precious gifts."

Singing The Song of Life: One Woman's Symphony is dedicated to my wonderful and dearly loved husband, Ari.

Thank you for the gift of freedom which allowed me to follow my dreams and become the woman I have always wanted to be. Thank you for your valuable editing suggestions, considering you never spoke a word of English until you came to America.

Without your unconditional love and devotion this book may have never been written.

You are truly the love of my life.

Acknowledgements

To my mom: Thank you for always being my best friend, forever loving, and my greatest fan.

To my sister: Your strength and courage have been amazing. I'll always love you.

To my daddy: Thank you for giving me the freedom to learn and live my life the hard way; it was worth it.

To my best and dearest friend Jennifer: Thank you for 32 years of our indestructible friendship.

To my precious Prince, who gives me the greatest gift every day; unconditional love.

Thank you, Marilee, for persuading me to meet Ari that unforgettable night. You brought two lives together that have made their world a better place.

In memory of Rabbi Stein
1920-2003
Rabbi Stein was the most wonderful, compassionate, and the kindest man I had ever known.
He will forever be missed, and will always hold a special place in my heart.

Thank you to my extended family, The Wingers
for giving me the family life I have always wanted.

A special thanks to Dr. Kaplan,
who will always remain in my mind's eye.

Thank you to my favorite cousin Kathy,
for always being there for me
and answering my questions.

Thank you, Janie and Sheila, for sharing
your children with me.

Thank you, Nanny Kayla,
for your love and care for Prince.

Thank you, Nancy McCurry,
for helping me enhance my writing skills.

Thank you, Angela Boss,
for your editing and endearing words of support.

Thank you, Diane, for your editing skills.

Thank you, Sarah, for your friendship,
support and inspiration.
Your gift as an artist portrays your inner beauty.

Thank you, Lynn Rosen-Bright for being there for me.
Your wonderful friendship and extraordinary editing
skills have meant so much.

Disclaimer

Out of respect for their anonymity, I have changed the names of the people who appear in these pages to protect their privacy. This is my memoir, and the events and experiences are all true and faithfully written based on my memory and to the best of my knowledge.

Table of Contents

Chapter Title	Performed by	Page
1 *Dream a Little Dream of Me*	Mama Cass Elliot	1
2 *Don't Rain on My Parade*	Barbra Streisand	23
3 *Going to the Chapel*	Dixie Cups	45
4 *Material Girl*	Madonna	58
5 *Your Heart Will Lead You Home*	Kenny Loggins	82
6 *Somewhere*	Barbra Streisand	94
7 *Solid as a Rock*	Ashford and Simpson	107
8 *That's What Friends Are For*	Dionne Warwick	112
9 *Help*	Beatles	121
10 *Papa Was a Rolling Stone*	Temptations	131
11 *Sound of Silence*	Simon and Garfunkel	135
12 *Never Thought I Could Love*	Dan Hill	155
13 *Grow Old With Me*	Mary Chapin Carpenter	174
14 *We are Family*	Sister Sledge	186
15 *Celebration*	Kool and The Gang	200
16 *Love and Marriage*	Frank Sinatra	216
17 *Bad Case of Loving You (Doctor, Doctor)*	Robert Palmer	226
18 *I Hear a Symphony*	The Supremes	251

CHAPTER ONE

"Dream a Little Dream of Me"

Mama Cass Elliott

As usual, I was sleeping like a dead person re-entering dreamland as I did every night. However, this night was different and so was this one particular dream that felt so real. It was so serene, and nothing was odd or frightening. Everything I could see and touch made perfect sense to me. The beach was loaded with white sand, which felt cool to my sunburned feet. The crystal blue ocean waves were elegantly moving in the slowest of motions towards me, and then, gently drifting afar with the white tips of the waves moving further into the distance.

As I walked along the beach absorbing the beauty, two young girls appeared, one on each side of me. One was a blonde and the other was a brunette.

Both girls had ponytails swaying back and forth as the wind floated through their hair. The girls each took my hand and walked as we began to sing the song "Fly Me to The Moon. In other words, hold my hand." Unexpectedly, and out of control, I noticed the blonde girl was crying her heart out.

"What's wrong, honey?" I asked.

"I'm so depressed, life can be so yucky. I'm so sad, so sad. How can I sing a song, when I can't even go for a walk along the beach without crying?" she answered.

Wrapping my arms around her and squeezing tightly, I gently sang:

"Sweet dreams that leave
all worries behind you."

When I finished, I added, "If you sing the song of life and truly believe in yourself, you will no longer be sad."

It was the simplicity of that dream in April 2004, that not only woke me from my sleep with a rapid heartbeat, but also awakened a compelling desire in my soul to write this story, my story. Though it appears to be normal on the surface, it is far from normal, and, as I write these words, I have discovered that each event from my past has helped me to survive the experiences that have molded me into the stable and strong woman I am today - fabulous at fifty.

Born in Detroit, Michigan, I was welcomed by fun-loving spoiled Jewish parents, Jacob and Rhonda Weitzman. My mom had been born in Cleveland, Ohio, and she attended Ohio State University for a short time. She was involved in a sorority and loved the excitement and camaraderie of it all. Her zest for life and the determination to have fun carried her through the hard times. She is a stunning woman and a definite head turner. Mom is 5'7" (*she'd kill me if I mentioned her weight!*), a natural brunette with gorgeous hazel eyes, extremely high cheek bones, full voluptuous lips, not a wrinkle in sight, and a mile-long smile. She has beauty inside and out, and she gets more beautiful as time goes on.

My dad was from Detroit, Michigan. I really don't know much about his past except for he was the oldest of three children, came from a wealthy family, had a controlling mother, and was spoiled rotten. He was very good looking and, according to my mom, he was a real player with the ladies. He was never without a pipe hanging from his mouth, and his true loves were golf and bowling. After my parents met at a Jewish dance, they married six months later in 1951. After a couple of years of living the good life, they decided to start a family. But they didn't realize that having children doesn't come with a how-to manual. December 1, 1954 and hoping for a son, my father missed the birth of his first child, me, because he felt the bowling league needed him more. Fourteen months later, eager for his son's arrival, dad was, once again, nowhere to be found when my little sister Lori was born.

"Dori, here's your new baby sister," Mom said as she placed Lori in my arms. *Maybe she thought I was the mommy.* Being a December baby, my birth sign is Sagittarius, aiming my bow and arrow high into the future. We lived in a nice three bedroom colonial, in the heart of Detroit, surrounded by neighbors with whom my parents had a lot in common.

Our little happy life lasted until I was four years old. It was riddled with sadness from that day forward.

3

It was obvious to me that my parents were emotionally and financially spoiled, and they couldn't cope with one another in life's trials and tribulations. I was just a little girl, yet I was forced to listen to the piercing sounds of screaming between my parents.

"I can't live like this anymore! Damn you Jacob! All you care about is golf! The bills have to be paid! You can't earn a living when you're on the ninth hole, every day!"

"I have good men running the business. Don't worry Rhonda, everything will be fine. You're just worried you won't be able to go out on Saturday nights anymore! All you care about are your girlfriends!" Dad would scream back. This constant fighting led to the adrenalin racing through me; covering my ears just didn't help.

I had the same feeling you get when you see flashing lights from the police car in the reflection of your rear view mirror, and you don't know what you've done. *Why would anyone want to get married?* The hostility and the death-like look on my mom's face was rapidly manifesting within our family unit. At the innocent age of seven, I became their rock and confidante, long before my body and mind caught up. I never had much of a childhood, nor did I enjoy the innocence of youth because due to my parents' failure to perform as responsible adults, I was forced to be a grown-up early on and offer emotional support for them. For example, my mother would constantly ask me, "What should I do, Dori? My life is a travesty (*whatever that means*). Should I leave your father?"

Growing up without the financial security my parents were accustomed to was tough. They were "suddenly broke", with "no cash on hand." Though my grandparents fared well, they didn't equip my parents to be adults. It all began when my paternal grandfather Benny died. He left his very successful tool and die business in good financial standing to his wife Lolly and his two adult sons, one of whom was my dad Jacob. My dad loved golf. Actually, he adored and worshipped golf. So instead of running my grandfather's business, he, along with his brother, decided to hire someone else to run the company for them, so dad could play golf. My mother Rhonda protested, but stood by my dad, more out of loyalty to the institution of marriage than out of her love for him. Divorce was not common back then and my mother had also been raised by wealthy parents, so neither she nor my dad knew the meaning of working hard, which drove them further apart as time progressed. Six months later, the men they hired to handle the business disappeared along with the files, equipment, and all the money.

Suddenly, our lavish life came to a shocking halt, and things had to change. My dad, who never had any skills, couldn't hold a real job. My mom, in her devastation, was unable to face the reality of their situation. Though their extravagant lifestyle came to an end, she still wanted to keep up with the Joneses. This situation only led to more horrific fights over money, parenting, and their social obligations.

I was four years old when dad moved our family from our roomy single family home. It was located on a huge corner lot with many tall flowering trees and the greenest grass I had ever seen. The exterior of the home was all brick with green siding, which blended in beautifully with the landscape. I remember watching our gardener Griffin from my bedroom window. He kept the lawn so well manicured and I was always so glad to see him. Griffin was a happy soul, and he paid attention to me. My nickname was

Dorio. However, I knew this was all about to change the day I saw this huge truck that seemed to be a mile long in front of our house. I overheard my dad saying, "Rhonda, I promise you and the girls, moving into a rented townhouse is temporary, until I get back on my feet." Dad reassured her as he gently kissed her tense and crinkled forehead. *Oh how fun is this going to be?*

The apartment had two bedrooms, one and a half baths, living room, kitchen and basement. Mom furnished it with used furniture; nothing fancy, but it was home and we were comfortable. Unfortunately, the new residence didn't stop the creditors from calling us. Shortly after we moved in, Lori and I watched two big thugs come into our home and repossess the only television we had.

"Lori, I'm scared stiff," I whispered as I held my breath, bit my tongue, and watched these horrible men take away our only source of entertainment.

"Don't worry Dori, mom will get it back." She comforted me as if she were the older sister.

Dad was clueless about how to earn a living, but mom got a job in a fancy women's retail shop and continued to hold her head up high publicly. I felt a tiny dash of hope while witnessing the basis of her strength. She loved to live, and her zest for life and survival could not keep her down. The black widow of financial pain continued to dangle its legs over us, making the entire household miserable.

I vividly remember seeing mom standing alone by the kitchen window sobbing in horror while dad sat in the bathroom crying and feeling sorry for himself. She cried constantly, living daily with this tormenting fear of uncertainty, rage, and agonizing pain.

"Lori, they cry so much, I think my own tears froze up along the way. I feel like we're so alone."

"Knock it off, Dori. Your tears aren't frozen," she would say, trying to be strong.

Mom's beautiful face was sallow and discolored from the emotional pain that she was enduring. Her yellowish skin reminded me of a yellow traffic light blinking, as if to warn her of the things to come.

There was a time when I was so terrified from the sights and sounds of their ugly fights, I would run out the front door and scream at the top of my lungs, "Help someone, please come quick!"

I desperately wanted anyone with authority to come over and help me stop them from hurting one another. My voice was heard, and more than one neighbor came running over to end the chaos. My parents fighting would cease, at least for the moment.

My maternal grandparents still lived in the same house where my mom grew up in Cleveland, Ohio. Mom made sure we traveled by car, bus, boat, and, once in a while, we would fly in to see them, once or twice a year. *I wonder why dad never drives us to Cleveland?*

"Mom, how come dad never goes with us?" I asked innocently.

"Because grandpa gets very upset when he sees your father," she answered sheepishly.

My grandma and grandpa would shower Lori and me with generous gifts at every visit. I saw such a loving connection between them. However, mom was always very tense in their presence.

"Lori, I hate when mom gets like this. Why is she so miserable?" I would ask in a soft whisper.

"I guess because she is so unhappy and needs money," Lori answered honestly.

7

I felt a real sense of security because I had my grandparents to turn to for safety and comfort. But more than the gifts they gave us, it was the demonstration of their love for one another and the security they had found in each other that gave me hope that a loving marriage, mutual admiration, respect, and being the best of friends was possible for me, too. I remember listening in amazement when they would talk with one another:

"Are you hungry dear?"

"Yes dear," he would answer with a smile.

As she set the chicken soup down in front of him, she would say, "I love you dear; enjoy your soup. I made it especially for you."

"Thank you dear," he'd reply while reaching up to kiss her on the cheek. They were always exchanging loving words and living out the phrase 'to honor and cherish one another' each day of their lives. This made me feel somewhat connected and all my wants and needs were normal. Seeing my grandparents in a harmonious relationship, secure in their surroundings, conveyed to me the possibilities I could really have in my life. *Just because my own parents are miserable or my father can't support us, that doesn't mean the same thing will happen to me.* I knew then that I would spend the rest of my life searching for the right place for me.

As a small child, I did manage to find some joy outdoors. There was a playground where the townhouse was located where Lori and I would play for hours. There was also a pool with lifeguards who taught me and all the other kids how to swim. I really enjoyed being outside where it was peaceful. I learned I loved animals, and I developed the idea of planting a garden. However, where we lived there were only

8

visiting dogs, and you weren't allowed to plant your own garden.

I often brought home strays that I found, but could only keep them a short time before the management found out. Then the standard threatening letter of eviction would arrive, so of course they had to go, taking my heart with them.

"Daddy, where did you take my doggie?"

"To a good family, you don't have to worry."

"I don't believe you. If you're telling me the truth, take me there right now."

"Not today, but maybe we'll go next week," he said. Dad claimed to have found a good home for them, though next week never came.

I didn't ask for much, but I kept my dreams hidden in my heart, which helped me to look forward to living a life different from the one I had known. I dreamed of a husband who would love me and be my best friend. We'd own a home with a huge backyard, filled with our four kids playing with the family dog.

I was almost eight years old when mom finally considered getting a divorce, though she didn't follow through at the time. I can still remember Lori and me as we painfully watched dad lie in bed on Sundays either sleeping or crying.

"I wish he would take us to the movies, bowling, or out for a cheeseburger. Why doesn't he ever want to be with us?" I asked Lori.

"He's the laziest and the saddest person I have ever met," Lori said angrily.

"Do we have cooties or what?"

"No silly! He does," she answered, and we both started giggling.

Even though he was such a pathetic soul, I always wished he would spend any amount of time with me.

The next few years were hard on everyone; mom worked six days a week at the ladies' shop. She seemed to be getting stronger so she added cosmetics to her line of work. Though mom wasn't home a lot, she left us cereal set up on the kitchen table and a snack set up for when we got home from school. This was her way of showing us we were loved no matter what. In the meantime, dad dragged himself with his minimal skills to an insurance job a few days a week. When he would go to work, he wore his only black oversized suit, along with the same blue skinny tie and white shirt every single time. I knew when he left in the morning he would return later and be back in bed when I came home from school, never making a single sale. No matter what was going on at home, at school I kept my chin up and a smile on my face; something I learned from my mother.

I always believed G-d was there for me, perhaps in the corner of my bedroom standing guard like the angel in the Garden of Eden. I knew He was my friend and I had hoped I was His friend as well.

"Hi G-d, it's Dori! Make them stop! My heart hurts! I want my mommy and daddy to take care of me!" I didn't hear anything back, but I knew he heard me.

My parents finally got a divorce a few years later. While mom held us close, dad drifted further and further from our lives. Apparently still connected to the umbilical cord, he eventually ended up moving in with his mother in Florida, where she could keep him warm, safe, and secure.

Ten years later we were still in the same rented townhouse. I was fifteen years old and starting my freshman year in high school. Lori was 13 years old and in the eighth grade, which was junior high back then. Lori is a striking beauty like mom; tall, thin, with long, straight, dark brown hair, and an olive complexion. We are complete opposites even though we're only 14 months apart and came from the same mom and dad. She is conservative and more reserved in her actions than I am. She always acted tough like nothing ever bothered her; therefore, I leaned on her a great deal, and we were inseparable. We were all doing pretty well as life moved forward except mom wasn't around much. She was always working hard to support us or out on the town with her friends. When she was home, the telephone was glued to her ear.

"Mom, come quick! Something is wrong with me?" I screamed from the bathroom one Sunday afternoon.

"Hold on a minute Evelyn, my daughter is having a problem." I overheard her say.

"What is it Dori, I'm on the phone?" She asked, looking at me as if I should know what's happening.

"I'm sick, look at my underpants!" I said, screaming and crying.

"Oh, Dori, nothing is wrong with you. Your period started and now you are a woman. Run upstairs and get a Modess pad out of the linen closet and you'll be fine." *Why don't you get it for me?*

"Aren't you supposed to slap my face?" But she didn't hear me because she had already walked away.

Even though she didn't have time to be the mom I wished for, she made sure we had food on the table and took us clothes shopping too. Mom took us to the major discount store, Tops 5th Avenue. She would yank

things off the rack for Lori and me to try on. When she really liked a look on me, she'd say, "Dori Darling, this outfit will be perfect for our trip to Mexico."
She made buying clothes fun and a memorable experience. Her positive attitude was stupendous. Although she wasn't around a lot, like a sponge, I absorbed as much of her as I could.

Having very little parental guidance, Lori and I grew up without any structure. Getting good grades didn't matter to my parents, and we soon learned that we had to fend for ourselves. The house was usually a mess, and we imposed our own curfews. Mom usually treated my sister and me like her equals. She placed an uncanny trust in us, and I didn't rebel. I was home by 11:00 pm, but Lori on the other hand, always came in much later. We didn't have a good man in our lives, which only made men more confusing. I was clueless, but one thing I did know; their anatomy was different.

As we grew older, Mom, Lori, and I remained very close. Our relationship was more like best girlfriends, rather than mother and daughters. I always felt loved by her; she listened to me and my problems and always treated me like my own person. Mom didn't have a lot of time to spend with me, but when she did it was ever so valuable. If I wanted to buy something special, she always found a way to split the cost with me, which made me appreciate her and my material possessions even more.

After celebrating my sweet sixteen, one snowy, blistery day in December, mom brought home her new man. With my sweaty palms, I nervously approached him to shake his hand. He said, "Hi, my name is Michael and I'm going to be your new dad."

Hearing those shocking words, I looked at this short, stubby man. I slowly turned away from him and my skepticism was in full force. His statement not only sounded stupid, it stung like a bee.

Apparently, mom hadn't learned her lessons yet. I had high hopes for a new stepfather and I knew right then and there I would never learn anything from this man because he was nothing more than a reflection of his own insecurities.

Around the tenth grade, I already knew in my heart that I was going to be on my own sooner rather than later. I just wasn't sure how I would do it. My school offered a co-op program where I could work part of the day and go to school the other part. My counselor found a couple of jobs for me to seek out and I was hired on the spot. During the week I worked as a cashier in a huge, well-known jewelry store. After a short time I became head cashier.

On Sundays, I worked at Temple Hadera, a reformed synagogue, as a secretary for the Sunday school, taking attendance and bringing in donuts. However, being in the temple had become much more than just a part-time job. This became my way of going to Sunday school and having my own private Jewish life, education, and family. I became very close with the head rabbi, Rabbi Stein, and his two sons during my three years of employment.

Max, the oldest son, who was four years older than I, was tall, with long dark hair. He was skinny, carried a guitar, and looked like a hippie. He had a crush on me and wasn't afraid to ask me out. I didn't think he was cute, but somehow I held out hope of some kind that I could eventually go out with him because he was the rabbi's son and a little wishful thinking was kind of exciting. I did go out for dinner with him once, thinking maybe I would like him if I tried hard enough. We went to a quaint Greek restaurant in the downtown area. There were a lot of old people sitting around eating and drinking. He insisted that I order the grape leaves, which were nasty. I didn't want him to know how much I despised the dinner and his boring company, so I excused myself for a few minutes and went straight to the ladies room to regurgitate. At that point I vowed not to eat grape leaves and to never go out with him again. The next few Sundays at work I just ignored him. I didn't know what to say or do. Therefore, I chose to take no notice of him until he finally got the message and left me alone. Little did I know, decades later he would reappear in my life.

I had a lot of friends in high school, both male and female. I had my own clique; I was everyone's best friend, yet there was something missing. I didn't have a boyfriend to call my own. I knew my girlfriends were sleeping around, which I thought was a terrible mistake, because they were ruining their reputation. My young, sweet girlfriends were taking their clothes off and standing, sitting, lying down or whatever, naked in front of a boy. And letting them feel their innocent breasts while their fingers did the walking in the depths of a warm apple pie. Oh my G-d, possibly letting those boys stick their stupid dicks inside them. That must really be excruciating, *I would never.*

I wanted to wait as long as possible before I let a man do those things to me. I wanted a boyfriend who really cares and who won't use me, just because it's the popular thing to do. But just the same, I still wished I had a boyfriend. At the time, I did have a crush on the star of the basketball team. His name was Joey Levine. We'd have lunch together everyday. I lived for our lunches, so we could eat and talk. He shared feelings about his girlfriend troubles and sought advice from me. I was always the "good friend" and never the "girlfriend". I had written him a love letter in our senior year, which I never did work up the nerve to give him. So I tossed it into the lake along with the dream of his being the one for me. I felt lost and alone, and I just wasn't good enough to have a boyfriend. I wasn't cool like my girlfriends who were cute and little while I was tall and thick. I was part of a clique, where I didn't fit in. I packed this painful experience away on top of all the others, which is something I was getting good at. Yet Joey will always hold a special place in my heart.

I learned years later he had gotten married and had two daughters, but then was stricken with cancer and died at the age of thirty-three. When I heard he was in the hospital I wanted to call him, but didn't because I did not know what to say. None of my girlfriends called me about the funeral, and I never could pay my condolences and say goodbye once and for all. I was so angry when I found out he had died. I felt like there were two deaths here. I was so mad at myself for not calling him when I had the chance, even if it was just to say hello.

High school was supposed to be a place for me to learn and grow. However, I spent most of my time sitting in class daydreaming or talking out of turn. I never got into any trouble because I had a great rapport with my teachers. I never did well on multiple choice exams, so they would allow me to take my tests in essay form. I had terrible study skills, too. But what got me through was my sincere gift of talk and my attitude toward trying so hard and being honest with my teachers. I always felt different around my friends, but it was my job to hide my insecurities. I didn't have the new clothes, my parents were divorced, we lived in a rented apartment, and I didn't have a boyfriend.

They all had new clothes, steady boyfriends, and both parents at home who owned their own house.

Graduation came quickly. I saved enough money to purchase my own cap and gown for commencements. After the ceremony, I invited all of my friends over for a huge party without any adult supervision. While saving money from working at the jewelry store I was able to pay for the party myself. At the same time, while pretending to be having a great time listening to the loud music and celebrating with my closest friends, I was so angry at my dad for leaving me. And angry at mom because she wasn't around either; she was busy working and building her social life. Then suddenly, I grabbed a bunch of unwrapped hard candy and threw it all over the living room, from floor to ceiling.

After graduation, I continued working at the jewelers to earn extra money. Each time I draped a beautifully cut diamond necklace over my hand to show the customers, I cherished the thought that one day I would be on the other side of the counter purchasing one of those beautiful diamonds for myself, instead of just selling them to others.

I applied and was accepted to Eastern Michigan University. I had applied for government loans and worked part time in a drug store to earn extra money. I began to have a taste for real freedom, to party hard and to make new discoveries about myself. However, I knew my greatest challenge was going to be how to survive. The harsh reality set in, that I had to fend for myself and depend on strangers to gain economic security and emotional strength. The government would help me with the cost of my education, men would teach me about intimacy, and friends would help me grow. At the time, this was acceptable to me because

I didn't have a choice. But the most important thing about my college years was meeting my roommate Jennifer Shaw, who later became my best friend.

I also learned a lot about men in college. My first boyfriend was Tony. He wasn't Jewish, but was he a cutie, *oy vey!* However, that didn't matter. He was such a wonderful guy. He approached our relationship at a cautious and steady pace. He knew I was still a virgin at the age of eighteen. I was terrified at the thought of losing my virginity with all the emotional and physical changes that would happen.

I was afraid of the excruciating pain and mess afterwards, getting naked in front of him and feeling major guilt for passing judgment on my high school girlfriends. But Tony was gentle and never forced himself on me. And taking it slow was the key. My own actions showed me that playing hard to get would make me different, and I wouldn't be labeled as an easy lay.

My conflict came to an end when Tony invited me up to his dorm room, where he had a bottle of Chianti and a six pack of beer. The song by Chicago, 'Colour My World' was blaring from the record player. *So this is French kissing, those French people are brilliant.* After making out for what seemed like hours of enjoyment, he gently removed my clothing and began caressing my innocent body with his warm hands and magical tongue. *So far, so good.* Tony laid me on his bed and, in what felt like slow motion, he entered me and I began to cry. *It's not a stupid dick now!* Tony held me and said with assurance, "You're alright honey! I love you, Dori."

My tears weren't tears of sadness, but tears of tremendous release of past judgments and the conflict I had been having with myself. The woman in me was born that day and I will never forget Tony as long as I live.

My mom and I never talked about sex; it was strictly taboo in our household. When I approached mom with any questions, her comment was always the same. "Dori, when you're 21 years old, I'll answer any questions you have." She would gently kiss my cheek and walk away. Sex was so confusing. However, because Tony was so understanding and tender with me, I was able to open up my mind and body to sex and intimacy, something I have never known. My feelings for Tony began to grow deeper and I looked at him and my other relationships with a lot more meaning. I had always related to the act of sex as dirty, but sharing intimacy and expressing my feelings in a physical way with someone I loved freed me from my inner self.

Being away at college gave me the freedom to come into my own. However, I was completely lost on the journey of education and career. I seemed to change my major every week. I was eighteen and had no idea what I was good at, what I wanted to do, or, for that matter, how I would do it. They—whoever they are—say going to college is the next step after high school. I didn't have a passion for my education, I never had. My dream was to have a secure home life with a husband, house, kids and a dog. I never wanted a career or to be the CEO of any given company. The only thing I knew how to do was to maintain my life to the best of my ability. I realized I didn't need another PHD because I already had one, Poor, Hungry and Determined.

Jennifer left college after one year, but we remained friends, and she visited often. After two years of partying and being independent, perhaps staying at college was not practical. Discussing this with mom, we decided together it was time for me to return home and get a job. I had two years of government loans I used for my education and my expensive partying, which had to be paid back.

Mom's *Tsores* (troubles) continue

I struggled with the thought of moving back home with mom and my step dad Michael. After they were married, he, mom, and Lori had moved into a new apartment large enough for me to move into as well. He worked all the time selling traditional furniture, which was a plus in my eyes. Yet, he was very controlling over mom. Moving back home proved to be a mistake. She still seemed to be depressed and crying, as she did before my real dad had left. Michael became very possessive, and demanded her attention at all times.

"Rhonda, get off the phone, stop wasting your time with your friends!" She would hang up like a scared little girl. I would constantly overhear him say, "Don't worry so much about the girls, I'm all you need!"

When it came to furnishing their home, she had no input whatsoever. He would have his company deliver the ugliest sofa ever seen, along with fancy tables and frilly lamp shades to match. I could see how mom got depressed just looking at it. Money was also an issue with him. He supported her by paying the rent and the utilities; however, he would cut up her credit cards right in front of her and limit any spending money she would need for necessities. Financially helping my sister and me was simply out of the question, and, when she did, mom had to hide her generosity. Not only did he keep her dangling from a thread, his vicious temper began to surface. He began to display his rage and anger verbally and physically. There were nights when Lori and I were in our bedroom, where I squeezed the pillow so hard covering my ears so I couldn't hear mom screaming and crying in terror.

"Lori," I whispered. "My insides feel like lightening is stabbing throughout my body, and my chest feels heavy like there's a typewriter sitting on it." Suddenly, Lori said in a piercing scream, "Shut up!"

Over the next few weeks, we were all living in fear of him. Mom began to lose faith and trust in him when he hit her with a closed fist because of petty jealousy. Yet still she remained in the complicities of it. The clincher for me was when this crazy man demanded that my seventeen year old sister and I pay rent to live at home.

"I'm so sick of this, Lori!" I yelled.

"Me too Dori, I'm so scared!" Lori replied.

"Let's get out of here; we'll do fine, okay, Lori?" I said nervously and she barely agreed.

"I don't want their problems anymore; they aren't mine or yours!"

"Me neither!" She responded in a bit stronger voice. So we decided that if he wanted us to pay rent we'd live on our own and not be controlled by him or live in such turmoil.

"Are you ready to be on your own?" I asked her.

"Yes, the only problem is I quit my job because they wouldn't give me the time off to go on my high school trip to Florida and I really want to go. Don't be mad, Dori." Lori pleaded.

"Are you kidding me? OK, just go have fun and I'll help you find a job when you get back. I was just curious Lori, what do you want to be when you grow up?" With her quick wit she replied, "I don't really care; I just want peace of mind!"

While Lori was away having the time of her life, I was on a mission. I contacted the landlord, who was a friend of the family. He owned a huge apartment complex and after telling him our sob story, he generously said, "I'll wave the security deposit and reduce your monthly rent."

"Perfect, I will never be able to thank you enough."

My search was over before it got started. When I looked around the empty apartment, all I saw were a few thirty gallon garbage bags filled with our clothes, not a stitch of furniture, and an empty fridge; I went into shock. In the back of my mind I had always hoped that my real dad would call to check up on us, but the phone call never came. I knew at that moment I had to dig deep inside myself to persevere without any help from my parents. At the young age of nineteen, I was so terrified to be on my own, but this was something I would add to my pile of insecurities and learn to live with. I also felt there would be obstacles, but more than that, I knew my life could be an exciting ride and I only had to be brave enough to take the first step.

After three short years of marriage and experiencing fighting, physical and emotional abuse, mom filed for divorce for the second time. She called me to help her move out the rest of her personal belongings, and, believe me, I was scared to go over there. I was relieved when I noticed a huge, muscular bald man dressed as a security guard, standing tall in the living room. Mom quickly introduced me to Big Joe.

"Mom, why do we have to go through this?" I asked.

"I know Dori, I'm so sorry," she answered nervously.

"Mom, please let's hurry!" I said urgently.

Michael fought her once again, only this time he begged for forgiveness.

"Rhonda, please don't divorce me! I'll change! You know I love you and the girls! If you divorce me, you won't get my Social Security!"

"I don't need or want your Social Security!" Mom said in anger. She continued with the divorce proceedings.

But will my mother ever learn? Why does she keep handing her life away? Didn't mom think she was good enough? I guess the thought of having a man, any man, was better than being without one. Her reliance on the wrong men created a wasted life filled with chaos and incompatibility and why didn't we have a dad? I had so many questions and no one to answer them.

Their day in court arrived and Michael continued to beg her not to go through with this and the divorce was final.

CHAPTER TWO

"Don't Rain on My Parade"

Barbra Streisand

My first corporate job was with a fantastic company called Evan Tours. The president of the company knew my parents socially. I filled out an application and was hired on the spot, a rare gift from my parents. Mr. Evan was the founder of group travel at reduced fares on chartered flights, which included the Caribbean, Europe, and the United States. My entry level position started in the Operations Department. This was where all passenger lists were finalized prior to every departure. I was only nineteen and eager to learn as much as I could in the shortest time possible.

I planned on making myself available to every department head, hoping for a promotion. There were many areas of interest, such as reservations, group sales, a retail travel agency, and a private travel club called International Travel Club. There was a lot to choose from and nothing but time and energy to attain my goals. Everyday, I punched in on time and punched out with overtime. Always smiling and friendly, I offered my assistance to everyone and anyone I came in contact with.

After two fast-paced years, my gears went into overdrive, when I accepted my latest promotion as supervisor of the reservations department. There were thirty-five agents under my direction. This was tough at first because I had to earn their respect. My good job was becoming a great career that I loved and felt very passionate about, a very rewarding feeling. When the company lost their department manager of the reservations department, her immediate boss knew I was qualified for the job; however, instead of offering it to me, they brought in a forty year old man from London, whom I had to train.

After Lori quit her job to go to Florida for her high school graduation, she came back happy and no cash on hand. Having our own apartment, I was getting pretty nervous. She tried to get another job, but without success; therefore, I offered her a job at Evan Tours. My job was very exciting and why not have my sister there to share it with? I was able to travel all the time. One thing my career did afford me was the opportunity to travel extensively. I also developed excellent business skills and good time management, which I never thought was possible. All these valuable lessons were carried into my personal life, too. I received more of an education on the job than I ever received in school. My game plan was to take full advantage of my travel benefits, figuring I would never be able to travel like this again. Mostly alone, I traveled throughout the United States, Mexico, the Caribbean, and parts of Europe, having the time of my life. However, cruise ships were my favorite. Every time I traveled on a cruise ship, I would go to the rear of the ship and sing Barbara Streisand's song "Don't Rain on My Parade." When I sang that song I felt as if the words were meant just for me.

In Mexico City, I had an opportunity to meet and spend time with the former President of Mexico's grandson, Miguel Aleman. A handsome man with his full head of dark hair and a meticulous mustache, I couldn't take my eyes off him. *'Hello, Gorgeous.'* As I was traveling by bus to the different cities throughout Mexico, Miguel would show up and invite me to dinner, where there were no prices on the menu. After dinner we walked hand in hand and smooched a little until I said goodnight. The next day when I arrived in Taxco, as I was checking into the hotel, there was a note at the front desk,

"I'm waiting for you on the beach!"

I simply ran out the main door, carry-on and all. It was like in the movies, when we finally embraced. Miguel continued to lure me and I continued to keep my distance. However, the romantic attention was very tempting. My trip to the three cities ended in Acapulco where he wrote in toothpaste on my bathroom mirror, *"I will forever miss you."*

One trip to Acapulco, I took my mom as a guest and everyone thought we were sisters. It ended up that the younger men were attracted to her and the older men were attracted to me. We had a wonderful and memorable trip together.

Since leaving school, my friendship with Jennifer Shaw continued to grow. She was born in Queens, New York. However, she was raised in the Detroit area and

25

still had a slight accent. She had long straight dirty blonde hair, gorgeous green eyes and her body was a little on the thick side. She was a selfless human being with a fun-loving personality to anyone who became her friend. She had the gift of gab and was a great listener. It has always been very difficult for her to talk about herself and express her feelings. She is the eldest of three children and felt she couldn't do anything right in her father's eyes. She protected her pain with sarcasm and jokes by saying, "I'm still here aren't I?"

Money was always a scarce commodity with Jen. In fact when she would drive around in her run-down red Impala, she called it Big Boat. Her attitude was contagious.

We didn't socialize together with others, but we spent almost every Saturday afternoon *shpotzing* (shopping) for the latest styles. She never stopped asking me a million and one questions about my life. Sometimes, I would be out of breath just answering them. We talked on the phone almost every day, even discussed being roommates again someday. One of her constant questions would always be, "Dori, when are we going to take a trip together?"

"Soon, Jennifer. In fact I was thinking about London, England. Why don't you apply for your passport and see when you can take time off from work?"

She had landed a great job at Sinai Hospital with health and vacation benefits.

"Are you kidding me?" she asked excitedly. I'll apply tomorrow. Oh Dori, I love you! I'm so excited and I can't wait!"

After a few months of planning we were off on an unforgettable vacation. We shopped at Harrods department store and didn't miss a boutique on Carnaby

Street. At one point, I couldn't find her, yet right before I was going to notify missing persons, she reappeared out of one of the shops. She had been enjoying herself at Piccadilly Circus, relaxing and making new friends. But for my dear friend, her thirst to see the history and experience all the sights had to be fulfilled. We took a crowded and extremely hot tour bus on an all-day excursion, which I hated except for one memorable stop, the Westminster Cathedral, where Princess Anne was married.

"Hey look at me, walking down the isle like Royalty!"

"You're cool Dori!" she said sarcastically. One evening, we had a personal invitation to the Playboy Club, where I learned how to gamble before it was legal. *This is what I call entertainment!* We also spent time doing girlie things like getting our hair done at Vidal Sassoon.

As we were flying home on the stuffy crowded plane, Jen leaned closer and placed her hand on top of mine and said, "I had so much fun and I will never forget this trip as long as I live. Let's be best friends until we're old and gray."

I agreed and we grabbed each other for a loving bear hug.

From Sweet to Bittersweet

There were many wonderful vacations and learning experiences to follow, such as landing in Munich, Germany, where suddenly an engulfing sadness overcame me as my mind wondered at the tragic events that took place in that region. An overwhelming sense of grief flooded my very being at the thoughts of what happened to the people, my people, the Jewish people who had suffered unimaginable torment and loss at the hands of Adolph Hitler. No wonder we're a minority; over six million of the Jewish population of men, women and children have been destroyed. It is impossible to make sense of that.

This was the main reason I never wanted to go there but I promised myself to make the best of it. These thoughts raced through my mind like the sounds of hail crashing on-to the windshield during a violent thunderstorm. However, even though I was reminded of the Holocaust, it forced me to re-examine my own life. *What do I have to complain about?*

In my rented blue Corolla, I traveled to Austria via the fast-as-you-can-go autobahn. I shifted into high gear, pressing the pedal to the metal harder and faster until I reached 95 miles per hour. *Wow, what a thrill this is, can't do much sight seeing now! So what if I didn't have the Norman Rockwell family growing up!* Afterwards, I realized the only limits I had were the ones I placed on myself. So from now on, I will work harder at being happy and successful then I ever did before; even if it takes me the rest of my life.

My travels were mostly in the United States because I always felt safer and I liked being closer to home. I had been to Hawaii a couple of times before. The crystal blue ocean, the surfers and the magnificent tropical flowers take my breath away every time. It's hard to believe I'm still in America. However, this trip to Honolulu seemed to be different. It had a romantic flavor that was about to change the direction of my life. I traveled alone, more so than not, but I always befriended other single travelers. During nine hours of a grueling trip from Detroit to Hawaii, I met a group of single girls.

"Hey Dori, why don't you come to our hotel later and lay out and we'll have some Pina Coladas?"

"Sure, I'll see you around 2:00ish."

Later, lying out by the pool with my new friends, covered in sunscreen with zinc ointment covering my nose and cheeks, I heard this deep voice.

"I see you're working hard on your tan. Can I buy you a drink?"

How can he even talk to me with white gook on my face? Through my bigger than life sunglasses, my eyes met his icy blues.

"I'd love one, thank you." I said, smiling.

"Name it, Beautiful!" He demanded.

I ignored the big lump in my throat and shyly answered,

"A Pina Colada will be perfect."

The drinks arrived a few minutes later and he suggested with his sexy Australian accent, "Let's take those chairs at the far end of the pool; we'll have a bit more privacy."

Not saying a word, sucking in my tummy, I gracefully got up and glanced over at my new friends and winked. In unison, the girls said sarcastically,

"See ya later, Dori!"

Stephen was a professional rugby player born and raised in Sydney, Australia. He was extremely tall, well built, good-looking with blonde hair, a deep dark tan and gigantic shoulders. He set up the lounge chairs so close that they looked like they were glued together.

"Lay down beautiful right here next to me and tell me if I can spend every waking moment with you?"

He laid his muscular leg on mine and said.

"I want to spend as much time as possible with you.

29

Let me get to know you." *G-d he's cool, who is this man?*

What do you have in mind Stephen?"I asked

He reached over and grabbed my trembling hands, lifted them up to his tantalizing lips, and said, "Let me show you the time of your life. I know a lot of extraordinary restaurants and clubs."

While staring me down he asked, "Do you like to dance, darling?"

"Love it!" I said with a giggle.

"There's a fantastic French restaurant in Maui, if your game?"

And we began making plans for the entire week. While seriously ignoring good common sense, I found myself agreeing with all of it.

His charm was killing me! Our conversation had become heated and so was I.

"Stephen, this sounds so exciting! I can't wait, but right now I need to jump in the pool and cool off."

"I'll join you," he whispered.

After an evening of a yummy steak, lobster drenched in butter, music and drinks, he walked me back to my hotel, kissed me passionately goodnight and said, "I'll see you at 9:00 am sharp for breakfast. Sleep tight Dori, I will miss you!"

What a gentleman and a relief, but why didn't he try anything?

I slept like a baby that night dreaming about Stephen. The next morning during breakfast, he shared his ideas of a fun filled day in Honolulu.

"How does this sound, my darling? A day at the beach and an evening filled with good food, wine, and the best disco on the island?"

This darling stuff is working! Later that night after a few hundred spins on the dance floor, we grabbed our drinks and collapsed on a chair big enough for two.

"Darling, do you want to take a walk on the beach later? I have something to go over with you," he said.

"What about, honey?" I asked.

"Our Maui getaway, OK?"

"Are you serious? Are we really going? I thought you were just kidding me?"

"Do I look like a man who would be joking around?" he asked seriously.

"No! Not really. OK, please go on." I agreed to listen.

"We're booked on Aloha Airlines and we're staying at the Maui Regency with our own secluded suite for the night."

Obviously, time got away from us and we never made it for our walk on the beach. My insides were bubbling like boiling water, and I thought I was in love with him. The tropical island of Maui offered incredible beauty which included an endless number of hibiscus and palm trees. While inhaling the scent of paradise, I was simply experiencing the greatest high you can imagine. *Romance was screaming loud and clear!* Stephen carried me into our hotel suite; he pointed to our private heart shaped pool and said, "That's for you baby."

Oh my G-d, this is like a honeymoon, but we forgot to get married! Later that evening, we hopped into a cab and I asked, "Where are we going?" *Man of my dreams.*

"Tonight, I'm taking you to the best French bistro on the island," he said with excitement.

"Sounds great," I said, thrilled out of my mind.

After we were seated, the waitress came to take our order, and Sexy Stephen asked, "May I order for you, darling?"

"Of course you may, darling." *Did I just say that?*

"My lady will have the duck l'orange with all the trimmings, in fact make that two. Thank you, Madam."

Dinner was luscious and so was he. After a few glasses of wine and a superb meal, we rushed home to make passionate love all night long. Early the next morning, while he was still asleep, I stepped outside and sat by the heart shaped pool that we had enjoyed just a few hours ago. *I can't go home! I don't want to go home! My passport is valid, I'm moving to Australia. I'll find another great job. I want to watch this Aussie play football or whatever they call it. I love him and want to be with him. I'll figure something out.* After a scrumptious breakfast of quiche and croissants, we headed back to the main island. Of course he didn't know my intentions.

While I was honeymooning in fantasy land, upon my return, the final hotel bill arrived; they had slipped it under my door. As I was scrutinizing my charges, I was startled by the ring of the telephone.

"Hello, my darling what are you doing?"

"I'm packing to go home, my plane leaves in just a few hours and I don't want to be on it. Take me back with you! I know I'll love Australia!"

"Don't cry. I'll tell you what, why don't you finish packing your things and meet me in my hotel lobby in one hour? OK?" He said, trying to calm me down.

"Alright, I'll be there." I said, sobbing.

I was crying so hard, I couldn't see straight. His hotel was in walking distance from mine, so I dropped my bags off at the valet desk in the lobby located on the main floor. I flew out of the double doors at high speed and ran down the main street as fast as I could, breathing heavily. *Those damn cigarettes.* There he was standing in the lobby of his hotel waiting for me. He appeared stunned to see me crying so hard and gasping for every breath.

"No, you must go home. I'm no good for you," he said as he held me close.

"What! Why would you say that? I've never been happier in my life! You made my heart sing and now there is no song!"

"I'm no good; you must go home," he repeated lacking any and all reason.

Without any sound answers from him, I fought for a few more minutes to no avail. He walked me back to my hotel to pick up my bags and watched me board the shuttle bus headed for the airport. As I dragged myself on to the bus, I fell into an empty seat by the window waiting for me. As the bus slowly pulled away, I placed one hand on the window and held tissue in the other to comfort my swollen and drenched eyes which were glued to his baby blues until his face faded away into the blurry distance. I never heard from him again.

It took me a few weeks to get over my honeymoon in paradise. I even took a week-end trip to Las Vegas to make me feel better. Little did I know, I would gamble like a fool and not be able to break my losing streak. So I bought myself a music box from the hotel's gift shop. It was a replica of a baby grand piano and now I had something tangible to show for my losses.

I was back to the office on Monday and happy to be there. Work was my solace, and at least I was good at something. Later that evening, I planned on calling mom to hear her soothing voice. Even through her own troubles, she was always there for me. Later that evening after a quick bite, the phone rang. It was mental telepathy and her timing couldn't have been better.

"Hello. Hi, Mom, I'm so glad it's you."

"Hi, Dori darling, how are you feeling?"

"Much better thanks, I'm over it. I've been doing a lot of thinking."

"What about, Dori?" she asked gently.

"I've made a decision, Mom. I never thought of myself as a career woman, but my job means every-thing to me and I'm finally good at something. It is teaching me how to prepare for the future. Especially in time management, organization, administrative, as well as witnessing the conversion from a manual system to technology. I now know how to operate a CRT (Cathode Ray Tube). That alone is a phenomenon in itself."

"You're right Dori, please go on."

"This job has given me strength and confidence, which is hard to come by these days. It has provided a much better education then I could ever have dreamed of in college. And the truly ironic thing is that I was paid to learn."

"Wow, Dori your eyes seem to be wide open."

"Yea, Mom they are. There's one more thing I realized."

"What's that honey?" she sweetly asked.

"Work agrees with me, men don't!"

She laughed and said, "You're only twenty-two years old, you have plenty of time."

"Listen, Mom, I used to think all I wanted to do was get married to the perfect man and build a loving family. All of it, the house, four kids, and the dog, will just have to wait."

It was then I vowed that I would not marry until I was twenty-five years old and for now I would travel and enjoy life until I'm ready to settle down.

"Does that make sense, Mom?"

"Yes, Honey. You're so wise and I love you very much!"

"Thanks, I'll talk to you tomorrow, I love you too."

After working for a few years, I was able to start a small savings account and establish some credit. I knew somehow in the back of my mind that credit cards and savings accounts were going to be my best friends. Even if there was only $50.00 in the account, it was there for emergencies. The credit cards allowed me to have the freedom to spend more money than I had, not realizing they had lulled me into a false sense of security.

After five successful years at Evan Tours, my supervisor Ernest called me into his office and gently broke the news.

"Dori, I'm sorry to be the one to tell you this; we are laying off 80% of the employees. And since you are so valuable to us, we're offering you a choice. You may take the lay off now with benefits or wait until the end."

"You're what? Why? I don't understand!"

"Don't cry Dori, it's been a great run! You have a fantastic future ahead because you are good at what you do." *Thank G-d, Lori had already come and gone.*

"I guess I'll go now!"

"I think that's wise, because we are sending you and a few others on an all-expenses paid trip to Hawaii, and you will receive three months severance pay. I hope this gesture of appreciation makes an adverse situation a little bit easier to swallow," my almost ex-boss said.

"I'm trying to absorb all of this Ernest, but thank you for being so generous."

Six months later, the company closed permanently. Unfortunately, the people that worked until the end received nothing.

After the loss of my job I thought would never end, I had a new position with another well known travel agency. The funny thing was, I had no sense of direction, yet I was selling airline tickets and tour packages. One client called in need of a round trip ticket from Detroit to Denver and on to Syracuse, New York. After taking all of his pertinent information, I said, "Your ticket will be ready after three this afternoon."

"Where are you located?" he asked, planning to pick up the ticket himself.

"We're on Orchard Lake Road, in between Twelve Mile Road and Thirteen Mile Road, on the right hand side of the street."

"Are you on the east side or west side?"

"I just gave you the exact directions; we are on the right side of the street." I repeated.

"How can I buy an airline ticket from you when you don't even know where your office is located?" he insisted.

"Don't worry, sir, I'm not flying the plane."

He laughed and said, "I will pick it up later today, thanks, Dori."

At twenty-four years old I was having fun being single. It was a time to be curious and very daring. I was always willing to try new things without looking at the consequences. I loved the disco craze, and Jennifer and I went dancing at least three times a week. Club O was the place; it was like my living room filled with old and new friends, especially some bad and fast moving cool guys. I always believed everyone was nice and trustworthy, but I was bored with the nice boys. I was pretty wild, drinking, flirting, and, according to Jen, sometimes even disappearing. Jennifer would threaten me, "Dori, if you ever leave without telling me, I will call missing persons!"

"Take it easy; I know what I'm doing."

At one point I took singing lessons, which I really enjoyed even though I couldn't sing. The first song I learned was in Italian, which I was told would help me learn to carry high and low notes. Feeling encouraged, I went all out and rented a piano so that I could practice at home. But that was short lived because I couldn't afford to keep this hobby going. Everything always seemed temporary in my life.

One Saturday afternoon, Jennifer and I went to a place called Tally Hall. It was a local mall that consisted of a food court, specialty shops, and entertainment booths. They had a professional sound booth where you could sing and record your own song. My selection was "New York, New York." Jen came into the small sound booth with me and sat on the floor and cracked up laughing because I couldn't sing. I still have the tape today, including her laughter in the background.

Another fun thing I did was register with a local talent agency to earn extra money. I was immediately called for a job and hired. It was a live "Gong Show," shown every Sunday evening in a sleazy club in Riverview, Michigan. I was hired to be The Mistress of Ceremonies. Without any professional training, I opened the show wearing a long gown, warmed up the audience and introduced the Master of Ceremonies to the theme from *Star Wars*. I was a natural. I had many costume changes throughout the show and did small bits in between the talent contestants. In one bit I was a little old lady on a park bench similar to the show *Laugh In*. In another bit I was a naughty nurse. All and all it was a great time and provided me with a creative outlet that I wanted.

About a year later, when I asked for a raise in pay, my boss declined claiming he couldn't afford it. I had to quit; it was just too far for me to drive. Ever since this experience, I have remained a frustrated "ham". I know now, if I had had the right encouragement and a little direction, I could have chosen to study acting or attend a college that specialized in dramatic arts. A few years later I did attend an acting class, but that too fell by the wayside due to insufficient funds.

Drugs were huge during the 70's. When there were parties held in psychedelic basements, where everyone was smoking a joint or whatever, I chose not to participate because I couldn't handle the feeling of being high and out of control of my thoughts and behavior. Drugs were not a part of my life, but due to peer pressure, I created my own way of fitting into the drug scene. I would take the joint and reverse it in order to blow a shotgun of smoke into my friends' mouths. I continued to hang around my druggie friends and did have the urge to try the hard stuff, but for some strange reason, I never got past my first attempt.

In 1977, I decided to run for Miss Michigan in the state beauty pageant. There were only three requirements; the contestants had to be single, a resident living in the State of Michigan, between eighteen and twenty-five years old. *Thank G-d, I don't have to sing!* I met the requirements and thought it sounded like a lot of fun, but I didn't have the extra money to enter the pageant. During this time, I was dating another too-cool-for-me guy. His name was Raymond, and he was quite the generous man. He thought this was a great idea and supported me all the way.

"Dori let me sponsor you! I'll take care of all the entry fees; this will be fun for you and a pleasure for me."

"Really, you mean it?" I said sincerely.

Without hesitation, I accepted his offer. In my mind, I thought this would be a great experience and it wouldn't matter whether I won or lost. Mom, Lori, Jen, and a few close friends were there to support me. My knees were trembling like crazy as I walked down the runway in an elegant soft peach gown, with a sexy black bathing suit underneath (needed for a quick change), wearing black stilettos and a white flower in my hair. It was scary and fun all at the same time. I lost the pageant; however, I was a winner to me. Hidden deep inside me I had carried and been forced to protect layers of my deepest and darkest insecurities. *Wow, I'm not so afraid anymore, I can do this life! Obviously, if I can walk down a runway in next to no clothes in front of thousands of people, television personnel, and lose the contest to boot, I can do anything!*

"I'm gonna live and live now. Get what I want, I know how."

I truly believe I entered this contest to take charge and begin busting through my insecurities. *Just because mom was scared, doesn't mean I have to be.* This experience helped me to gain confidence and broaden my outlook on life.

It had been almost two years since mom divorced Michael, and she was doing a lot better. I hadn't talked to my stepfather since he demanded that my sister and I pay rent and we moved out on our own. He was never a real part of my life. Out of the clear blue, Michael called me and asked, "Dori, would you have lunch with me today?"

I immediately declined and said, "Oh that's so nice (*I lied*), but I have plans with a friend today."

As I hung up the phone in surprise, I wondered, *"What's that all about?"* Come to find out a few days later, Mom called and said remorsefully, "Michael is in the hospital and I don't know how much time he has left."

"Thanks for letting me know," I said unfeelingly.

So that's what lunch was all about; he treats us like garbage and now his guilt takes over. A small funeral was held with one person in attendance.

A few days later, following the funeral, Raymond took me out to dinner to cheer me up. But since I had no appetite, I drank my dinner in the form of wine.

"Dori, look, there's an old friend of mine, Rob. He's walking toward us."

"That's nice, Raymond." I continued to gulp down my liquid dinner.

"Dori, when Rob gets here, why don't you do something funny, like sit on his lap and act like you've known him for years?" Come on please," Raymond whispered. *I'm not in the mood for this!*

"Alright, I'll try." In a frail moment, I agreed.

"Hey, Ray, how ya doin good buddy?" Rob asked.

"Have a seat man," demanded Raymond.

The introductions were made and the small talk began. After a few long minutes, I abruptly got up and gently lowered myself on to his lap and said, "Hi, Rob, would you like a glass of wine?"

Rob looked amazed, as he stared into the windows of my soul, and said, "That would be great. It's so nice to meet you too, babe."

This act of friendliness resulted in a lot of laughter and Rob asking me for my phone number. *Who knew?*

In 1979, after working so many years for someone else, mom applied for a small business loan. She sounded so excited when she called Lori and me with the big news.

"Girls, we're approved! We got the money!" she said with delight and a smile in her voice.

Lori and I left our present jobs, and together the three of us opened Face Fitness Cosmetic Studio. Mom had created a first of its kind; a place where men and woman could have makeovers, drink champagne, listen to the sounds of the player piano and shop for French lingerie. This had become my second successful career and a very exciting time for all of us.

Saturday Night Fever with John Travolta was the hit movie that welcomed in the disco generation. As the silver ball continued to spin, so did my body and mind with Rob. Raymond was long gone, and my evenings were filled with my new man. Initially, my heart was with Raymond until Rob's tenacity took over. Our non-stop dating was taking over my life. He was fourteen years older than I, divorced twice, with two teenage daughters. *What a catch?* At first I was attracted to his outgoing personality and material possessions. The sights and sounds of the boat, Corvette, and the lakefront house represented the wealth that would eliminate my stack of bills and an unhealthy obsession that money conquers all.

However, as my feelings began to deepen, I felt love for this man. Obviously, he wanted to take care of me. Rob became very possessive, telling me what to do and how to do it. And he constantly said how much he loved me. Even though he had a bad reputation, his interest and care for me were something I couldn't resist and I kept going back for more. I wasn't too worried about what others had to say, because I would show them how wrong they were.

He was not the best looking man I had ever dated, but I was completely blinded by him because he seemed to really love me and wanted to take care of me, something I had never known. I was at a very vulnerable and impressionable age; therefore, I loved my new social life and that's what mattered. He would take me dancing all the time to different clubs, and we had great parties in his home, which was a real bachelor's pad. Life was fun, and I was quickly getting used to having this man sweep me off my feet. I was spending so much time in Rob's home that I kept asking myself; *why am I paying rent for my own apartment?* After about a year and a half of being inseparable, he said, "Dori darling, move in with me."

"I would never just live with you without a commitment," I said firmly.

"That's fine with me; I want you to be my wife. We'll have our wedding here at the house, outside on the lake. How does that sound, my darling?" He asked.

Without a second thought, I immediately gave up my apartment with Lori along with my independence to move in with him. It was during this time that the truth about his past began to surface. I met his first ex-wife, who was very hateful and bitter. His daughters and I became very close and I loved them very much, but soon learned they had many issues with him too. His second ex-wife was long gone and as our relationship developed, people that knew him would drop hints to me about his past and his bad reputation. But I was in love and refused to listen or accept the negative things that others had to say. In my heart, once we were married I planned on helping him become a nicer person and show him how to treat people with kindness and respect. Thus was the beginning of a very stormy relationship; I moved in and out of the house many times with my personal belongings thrown into plastic garbage bags. I would call my sister Lori, sometimes as late as eleven at night, hysterically crying, "Come get me out of here, now!"

Thirty minutes later, Lori showed up, honked her loud horn, while yelling, "Hurry up Dori!"

I barely leaped into the car as she sped away, while my head was hanging out of the window, screaming, "I still love you!"

While breathlessly running barefoot after the car, he yelled, "I love you too, my darling!"

"You guys are crazy!" Lori said, in disbelief, while shaking her head.

I moved back in with my sister until the next time. After I would leave him, a few days or a week would pass by, then I would bump into him, usually at a club, or he would start calling me. This happened on numerous occasions. Our physical chemistry brought us back together. I thought if I married Rob the insanity of our disastrous relationship, continuous break-ups and make-ups, would come to a screeching halt. We went to see Rabbi Stein at Temple Hadera to speak with him about getting married. He told Rob in a fatherly way, which endeared him to me, "Remember, Dori's father walked out on her and she will not let anyone walk out on her ever again! If you want to marry her, you must be sure."

"Yes, Rabbi, I'm sure," Rob assured him and squeezed my hand giving me a wink and a smile.

CHAPTER THREE

"Going To the Chapel"

Dixie Cups

In June of 1980 we were married; this would be the third time for Rob and the first for me. We had an outdoor wedding which I had planned myself. It was like a fantasy with yellow and white tents and a champagne fountain. With a flowered wreath on my head and ribbons spiraling down my back, I looked and felt like a princess. My gown was taupe in color and gracefully flowed to the ground. My dad was still nowhere to be found, which continued to sadden me, so I asked a friend of my mom's to give me away. Rabbi Stein married us, and I was a happy naïve little bride floating on a huge cloud of denial. Jennifer was my bridesmaid, standing by my side as always. I couldn't find her during the wedding celebration; she was always missing. I found out later she was out on the boat drinking champagne with Peter, her date for the evening.

The day after our wedding, we began our honeymoon at home. My husband prepared a beautiful breakfast that we shared outside on the deck overlooking the beautiful lake. I felt so happy that I had finally become "Sadie," a married lady; a title that came from my favorite movie *Funny Girl*. And I had realized my dream to marry at the age of twenty-five. After breakfast, while handing me a little pill he said, "Here darling, take this, you'll love it!"

Why shouldn't I trust my husband? So, I took the pill, no questions asked. About an hour later, I was running around the backyard trying to climb all the little hills. It was like doing the moonwalk in slow motion up in outer space. I became horrified and very frightened by how I was feeling.

"What was that pill you gave me?" I screamed.

"A happy pill," he said proudly.

"How could you?" I shrieked, almost gagging. At the top of my lungs, I screamed in horror.

"What the hell was in there?" I asked, coming to my senses.

Unfortunately there was no one around to help me. I got through the day; however, I felt so confused, miserable, and my head was throbbing so hard. This was supposed to be my honeymoon, not a living nightmare.

Our real honeymoon was scheduled about a week later. As the days progressed, I felt more and more comfortable living in the house with him. He enlarged the closet off our bedroom and designed a beautiful dressing area for me. We spent our time on the lake, having dinner on the boat. It was paradise. Love and marriage conquers all. Or so I thought.

We were off on our honeymoon for a three-day cruise to the Bahamas. The second day of the trip it rained, so we decided to see the movie *Grease* in the ship's indoor theatre. I remember listening very hard to the words of the song "Hopelessly Devoted to You," and I vowed to be a devoted wife to Rob.

After returning from our honeymoon, early one morning, while Rob was at work, I was straightening up the house and found some of his drug paraphernalia. I questioned it, but then brushed it off. This was just one more of the many red flags I chose to ignore.

As the days and weeks progressed, he became very possessive of me, and I began alienating my mom, sister, and friends, including Jennifer. He would scream at me if I talked on the phone to any of them. He didn't let me out of his sight. While we were home relaxing, if I would get up to do something, he would question my every move using less than a charming tone of voice. The anxiety level in my life was rising; things didn't feel right. Though he never hit me, often in a heated argument he would grab my shoulders and shake me terribly. After only four weeks of marriage, I knew something was desperately wrong. I could not deny the red flags any longer and felt stupid, naïve, and deceived. *Why did I think I could change him into a decent human being?*

One evening while taking my shower, I felt like a happy young bride once again. I walked out of my dressing area wrapped in a towel to see what he was doing and to give him a kiss on the cheek. I looked at him and stopped dead in my tracks when I saw he was relaxing in bed, watching TV with his hand resting on a gun. As my mind began to race I said to myself, "Don't panic, act normal and stay calm." My insides were in turmoil, and I was damn terrified for my life. I forced a smile and pretended everything was normal.

"Honey, what are you doing?" I tried to sound calm.

"I don't want anyone else to ever have you, and you will belong to me, forever!" He said with an eerie assurance.

"Honey, don't worry, no one else will ever have me; that is why I married you," I said, kissing him on the cheek and excusing myself to dry my hair. Petrified out of my mind, I walked slowly back into the bathroom and started to have flashbacks about how so many people had warned me to stay away from him. *What am I going to do now?* I can't tell one single soul about this horrific act of insanity, due to sheer embarrassment alone. I was also too petrified to leave him because I was afraid he would kill me. I felt so terrified and very much alone.

The day after, I went to work and when my mom would see me crying, she thought it was the stress of being a new wife and working.

"It would be a good idea, Dori darling, for you to take some time off and spend it with your husband," she comforted me.

If mom only knew! She gave me a big hug and a kiss and held me close, as I continued to cry in her arms, until my face was bright red and drenched with tears. I couldn't tell her or anyone what was going on because I was so ashamed that I had made an enormous mistake. *Why didn't I listen? I thought everyone was just a know it all!*

"Go home, Dori darling, and rest," she said.

"Ok Mom, thank you I will!" I agreed.

As time went on I realized that, due to the stress, I had developed insomnia and the taste of food was revolting. Now instead of eating or sleeping, I would pace the floors day and night. It wasn't long before Rob began noticing a dramatic change in my behavior. He began screaming and badgering me. My head began to hurt as if a sledgehammer was going wild on it. I knew something was dreadfully wrong with me.

"Today's the day we'll say 'I do'
And we'll never be lonely anymore."

I would stay home alone during the day and couldn't even dress myself. I would just walk around the house in my dark world, frightened to death in a daze. I still hadn't told anyone about the gun or the threat because I felt such shame over my decision to marry him.

One afternoon, more fearful than ever, I couldn't even answer the phone. After numerous tries, Mom began to panic when she didn't receive an answer. Suddenly, as I sat home alone and scared to death of my own shadow, the doorbell started to ring continuously. I realized this noise wasn't stopping until I opened the door. Out of intense fear, I cautiously approached the door, and peeked through the window. I let out a sigh of relief when I saw that it was my mother. She came in, we sat on the couch, and she saw something was terribly wrong. She begged me to pack up my things and come with her, but I refused.

"Mom, I can't leave him. I have to wait!"

"Wait for what?" she asked.

"I'm not sure what I'm waiting for."

I felt frozen stiff and was too frightened to leave.

"We are supposed to go to Rob's brother's house for holiday dinner in just a few days."

"Dori darling, you don't have to go!"

"Yes I do. He's my husband!" I argued, feeling an obligation, but unbeknownst to me her words were the key that would enable me to unlock the door of this prison that my marriage had become.

In September, about eleven weeks into the marriage, the evening of my escape arrived, and so did Rob's two lovely daughters. Little did they know that they were a *"mitzvah"* (a blessing in disguise); they came into the house dressed for dinner, and we were all going to drive together to his brother's to celebrate the Rosh Hashanah (Jewish New Year) holiday. I managed to get dressed and had my purse and keys nearby. I kissed the girls, grabbed my stuff, and then like a robot I walked toward the front door.

"I have to go, this isn't for me!" I said and simply, but nervously, walked out the door.

I felt relief for the moment because I knew Rob wouldn't hurt me or do anything in front of his children. I was shaking like a leaf and I felt very bad that I had to behave like this in front of his daughters. But it was my only way out. I drove straight to my sister's apartment that night, thinking about how my mother's words had been the key that unlocked my imaginary door that I thought was made of steel.

"No pill will cure my ill."

I barely could lift my hand to knock on Lori's front door. When I saw the only person I trusted in this world with her arms wide open for a long needed hug, I felt protected and out of harm's way.

"Come on in, sister. Your safe now," she reassured me.

"Lori, I can't feel my legs."

"Shut up, Dori," as she slapped my upper thigh.

"Ouch, that hurt!" I screamed.

"Well, I guess you can feel your legs," Lori said with a smile.

"Why don't you go to bed and get some sleep and we'll talk tomorrow. Mom will be here too."

"Thanks Lori for always being there for me, goodnight. I love you," I said weakly.

"I love you too. I'm glad this fiasco is finally over," She said firmly.

Lori was always tough and she never tolerated crazy behavior, especially with Mom and now me. She refused to go to my pity party and that gave me strength.

The next day, Mom came over and we had a serious coffee talk. Lori realized I had been through some kind of trauma, and Mom was crying. My clothes didn't fit; they were hanging on me as if I were a coat rack. I was hardly talking, and I was frightened to leave her house. I explained the entire situation in bits and pieces while they listened intently in absolute shock. Later that day mom took me to the doctor. I had lost over twenty pounds and hadn't slept in weeks. He suggested that I go to the hospital due to exhaustion and get a complete checkup to be sure nothing was medically wrong. Mom and Lori made arrangements to have my personal things picked up from Rob through my mom's attorney, Gene Hoffman. I didn't find out about this until later, but everyone was instructed by Gene not to tell Rob my whereabouts.

After sleeping a solid week hooked up to a slow drip of IV fluids, I began to get my strength back and was ready for a visit from my attorney. While recovering from my nightmare in the hospital, Gene came to visit me.

"A time to love, a time to hate."

"Please Gene, report him to the police and make him pay for all of my torment. Look where I am! This place is weird; I see a lot of strange people walking around here. Get me out of here, now!"

"Look, he stinks! He's trouble and now that you're away from him, stay away! You won't win! Dori, remember one thing, when you play with a skunk, you smell like a skunk! I'm going to get this marriage annulled so you can get on with your life! Agreed?"

"Alright Gene, I agree."

Right after my visit with my attorney, Dr. Denton walked in. He asked the usual how-are-you questions, while checking my vitals.

"Dori you're going to be with us for awhile, and I'm going to be seeing you at least three times a week. Is that alright with you?" I began to cry uncontrollably and said, "I guess so, do I have a choice?"

I was so angry I could've screamed. I felt trapped again in a situation that I had created. I believed Rob would take care of me and I could save him. *Why did I marry him? What's wrong with me? He should be in here, not me!* Throughout my life songs have helped me cope. I would sing and identify with the lyrics and knew I wasn't alone. "Hello Dori" to the tune of "Hello Dolly" performed by Carol Channing and "Turn, Turn, Turn" performed by the Byrds, echoed in my mind. After about ten days, I felt stronger and finally came out of my room and began visiting other patients, instead of just getting out for meals. I listened to them and realized they were a lot worse off then I was. It was during this time I found I had a greater joy in rescuing others who were suffering and I knew I wanted to help them. As always, I was trying to save everyone else who came into my life.

"A time to build up, a time to break down."

During my mandatory visits with Dr. Denton, he tried to make me understand what happened to my body and mind, although never explaining why they had broken down. However, he did say, "Your personal shut-down was a way of protecting yourself. Your attraction towards Rob was for all the wrong reasons. A man who is fourteen years your senior is more like the father figure that you starved for, rather than a loving husband."

"Dr. Denton, I thought I could change him, the way I never could change my father," I added.

During my stay, mom and Lori brought me a bunch of new pajamas and my tape recorder filled with my favorite songs. They gave me so much love and support. Without their constant visits, telephone calls and generosity, my recovery would not have been as quick as it was. I cleaned myself up, dusted myself off, and felt better than ever.

"Dori will never go away again."

About a month later, Mom picked me up at the hospital and offered to take Lori and me out for a family dinner to celebrate. When I saw where the hostess was seating us, I angrily asked Mom, "This is a nice Italian restaurant, why are we sitting on the bar side? Being serenaded by loud obnoxious music and a bunch of hungry single people drinking is not my idea of warm and fuzzy."

"Dori, I'm so sorry, I thought you would enjoy this," Mom said sincerely.

"There is a time and place for everything. I guess you really don't know how important family is. Lori and I aren't your single girlfriends, we are your daughters."

"Ok, Dori that's enough. Let's just eat and go home," Lori interrupted.

During dinner, I was extremely upset since Mom's priority was to be surrounded by other people because we weren't enough.

I was back to work with my family and going out with Jen, partying at Club O. Jennifer and I went everywhere together; we picked up where we left off before I had gotten married.

"I'm so happy, you're home. I was so worried about you and I missed you so much." Jen said lovingly.

"Me too, you. Forget about all that, let's have some fun instead. Why don't you meet me at the club around 7:00ish?" I asked.

"I'll wait for you in the lobby, I can't go in alone," she said.

"Yes you can, you're a big girl," I said.

"You Keep Me Hanging On."

A couple of weeks later, I was back at the club disco dancing with a male friend; we went back to our table to grab our drinks. While trying to cool off, suddenly my stomach felt as if it had fallen ten flights of stairs when I saw Rob walk up to us. I freaked out and dropped my drink. It splashed all over me, my friend, and the floor.

"That's my wife you're talking to!" His words reeked with intimidation.

My friend looked at me speechless and quickly ran off. I was about to turn and scream for help when he stopped me cold.

"Don't be frightened! I won't hurt you! I'm so sorry. I never meant to hurt you!" He kept repeating.

The waiter rushed over to clean up the mess, without saying a word. Though the divorce proceedings were in progress, I fell victim once again to the physical attraction and ended up leaving the club with him. We began to see each other again and, of course, I was ashamed to tell anyone.

On the day the divorce was finalized, Rob and I planned on going out to dinner and his attorney thought we were crazy for dissolving our marriage. Suddenly, I had a secret life that was difficult to hide from my sister, with whom I was permanently living.

"Where are you going?" she'd ask, concerned for my welfare. I made up a fictitious male name and a fake plan for the evening. She suspected something was up and eventually figured it out.

"Don't tell Mom or anyone for that matter! Ok, Lori?" I demanded.

"I won't, even if you're the biggest idiot that ever lived!" she yelled.

The dating game was fun for another few months. However, this time, the clues and bad behavior which I previously had chosen to ignore, were now quite evident. And they were hitting me fast and furiously. Realizing I could never change him or show him how to treat others with kindness and respect, I knew our sick relationship had to end. Little did he know, this was our last meal together.

"Dori darling, what do you want to do for New Years?"

"I can't start another year with you. Not even one more day. I have a new life to live and it doesn't include you. It's over!" I told him with nervous confidence.

"Don't do this, Dori! I love you!" he begged.

"Set me free, why doncha babe? Give your daughters a hug and a kiss for me and let them know how sorry I am that it had to end the way it did. Don't get up, I'll catch a taxi. *Zol zein gezunt* (Live and be well)." *Was that me saying all that?*

"You too, Dori darling, I'll always love you!"

My relationship with him finally ended naturally and without any harassment.

As I look back, up until then we never had official closure on our relationship. Surprisingly enough, he understood and let me go peacefully. Enough was enough. As my heart began to harden, I swallowed my tears and truly never looked back again.

Over the next few years, Face Fitness Cosmetic Studio was in full swing. Mom became a public figure, and Lori and I were so proud of her. She also created "Fashion Fever," a series of electrifying fashion shows with a disco flavor, which I produced, directed, and modeled in. However, working with family had its ups and downs. I still felt like something was missing. I wanted to be discovered for real. I would dream about becoming a movie star and relocating to California. I loved Los Angeles, along with the huge sign in the Hollywood Hills stamped in the corner of my mind. I would travel to LA as often as possible. Walking down Rodeo Drive was exhilarating to me. I loved seeing the movie stars while having lunch at the popular deli, Nate and Al's. I knew I wanted to be a part of this world and was ready to head to California to pursue my lifelong dream. In 1982, at the end of my last production with my mom's company, the Master of Ceremonies played the song, "California, Here I Come" for me and everyone wished me well in my future. I flew to Dallas, Texas to visit some friends before leaving for Hollywood. During the flight, I met one of the executives from Delta Airlines. We began talking and by the time the plane had landed, he had convinced me that I should get a job in the travel business in Dallas.

"You will have a number of job offers; please don't throw away all of your knowledge and experience," he advised.

When I arrived at my hotel, I walked into a beautiful suite with a desk waiting for me to conduct some serious business. After I was settled in, I called a headhunter listed in the phone book and set up interviews in the hotel's café. I invited my potential employers for breakfast because I knew I'd never find their offices; I have no sense of direction. All in all, I conducted about six interviews and secured several job offers.

The part of me that longed to be safe and secure accepted a great position that paid well, with all the benefits. It was a wonderful, secure job in the travel industry. I took it in lieu of traveling the risky road to Hollywood to be an actress. After a few days of visiting with friends, which had been the original reason for my trip, I flew back to Detroit to pack my bags for my latest destination: Dallas, Texas.

CHAPTER FOUR

Material Girl

Madonna

In February 1983, I said my goodbyes and set out for my new home in Dallas, Texas. My first room-mate, Marcy, was also from Detroit. I was able to build a stable life in Dallas, working for a national travel company in a supervisory position handling individual and group travel arrangements for large corporations.

Though I had come from a poor, broken home and a crazy divorce of my own, I was very proud of how I had turned it all around thus far. Through determination and perseverance, I set and attained personal goals to compensate for the missing pieces of my life. On a professional level I had achieved a lot for my age, but on a personal level I still had work to do. Life was pretty good; I spent my days working hard at my job and my nights dancing, eating Mexican food and drinking margaritas.

One Saturday afternoon, after a day at the mall with my former associate and friend Garrett, we had finished lunch, said our goodbyes, and went to our respective cars. Just a side note, Garrett had been under my supervision at Evan Tours and introduced me to an eye opening experience, the world of homosexuals. This was after I thought I had a crush on him, but he turned out to be a dear friend to me and became the brother I never had.

Unexpectedly, a man in a blue Chevrolet Malibu Classic pulled up next to my car and signaled to me to lower my window.

"How would you like to make $10,000 a week?" he offered. Even though this man was a total stranger, in my naive mind I thought he was going to change my life forever! He looked like a pretty conservative man with dark blonde hair, glasses, and a thin build, a real bookworm type. Not being cautious of strangers, I decided to listen to what he had to say.

"Yes, I'm interested; tell me more about this," I answered with dollar signs dancing in my head. He went on to tell me that his name was Tony Stevens and that he was holding interviews at Love Field airport right then.

"I can't go on an interview now! Number one, I'm dressed in blue jeans, which is not very professional, and number two, I have plans tonight."

"You look beautiful and nothing else matters," he said.

"Ok, but I want to take my own car and follow you to the airport," I replied.

My mind was more concerned with going out to the clubs that night with my girlfriend Bonnie.

"Tony, before I go anywhere, I have to get to a pay phone to call my girlfriend," I said anxiously.

"No problem, just follow me to a nearby telephone and then we'll head to the airport," he said, seeming to be so nice and considerate.

I called Bonnie and explained what was going on with this job interview and that I would be a little late.

"Who in their right mind goes on a job interview at 5:00pm on a Saturday night?" she yelled furiously into the phone and slammed the receiver down, causing my ear to vibrate. *What was her problem?* I remember shaking my head and thinking of how that poor girl had no adventure in her life. I vowed to call her later after she calmed down.

As I followed Tony to the airport, doubts came and went as I replayed Bonnie's comment, but ten grand is ten grand, and I figured it was too late to turn back now. I followed Tony through a private security gate as he signaled me to park my car. There was a beautiful navy and white Lear jet with the stairway already dropped down, waiting for me to enter. I walked slowly up the steep steps to the plane. The moment I entered, I immediately noticed the crew lying on the floor smoking substances that did not include a Surgeon General's warning on the label. Slam! Before I could turn around to see where the noise came from, the door had been slammed shut and locked behind me. I was being kidnapped! White slave market! *Oh why wasn't I a brunette?* I looked at Tony.

"Would you mind explaining this job to me, right now?" I asked trying to appear to be composed and in control, which was far from the truth. I took a deep breath and hoped he didn't notice how nervous I was. Tony went on to explain that he ran an escort service and my job would be to fly back and forth between here and Denver, Colorado twice a week while escorting his VIPs.

"Oh, so what are my duties?" I asked trying to play dumb and act interested so I would be able to leave this plane quickly and unharmed.

"During the flight, your responsibilities will be to keep my clients company. You are to dress very sexy and you must fulfill any sexual needs he or she may desire," Tony said with a carefree voice.

I was absolutely shaking all over. I felt as if a blender was chopping ice inside my entire body.

"Why don't you give me your business card and I will think about it and call you in a couple of days?" I said, confidently.

"No," Tony didn't agree. "Why don't you give me your phone number and I will call you."

I happily agreed and gave him my business card. The doors began to open, and with the crew indisposed by their activities, I took multiple wide-angled steps over these drugged out human bodies towards the door and down the steps that seemed ever so steep.

I broke into a run and was gasping for air as I reached my car. *Wow, Bonnie was right about him.* I got in and looked up to see him bending over with his face framed in my car window. I lowered it just enough for him to talk, when he began apologizing profusely.

"I'm so sorry if I offended you. You seem like a very nice person and I see this job isn't for you."

He offered to buy me a drink at a nearby hotel to calm me down.

"That sounds great," and I followed him to the hotel.

61

He's not so bad, after all. Bonnie was so wrong, there are decent people out there.

We went to the lounge at the Dallas Inn to talk and relax. He told me a little about himself, which seemed to strike a sympathetic chord in my heart. He went on to tell me that he owned this huge corporation, Stevenson & Associates, and that he did a lot of record promoting and had discovered many new talented artists. This was right up my alley. He also told me that he was a licensed pilot and owned several jets. He was no doubt very successful and enjoyed all the glitz and glamour life had to offer. Time flew, and I realized that it was nine o'clock. I was stunned by the time and realized that I had stood Bonnie up. Being the gentleman that he was, Tony walked me back to my car. *What an exciting and interesting guy he is.*

"You deserve a break! Are you making car payments?" he asked as he opened the door, while examining my Pontiac Fiero.

"Of course I am. Why?" I asked.

"Listen Dori, my secretary will telephone you tomorrow and request the name of your finance company and account number. Your cute little car will be paid in full, as soon as possible. Consider it an apology for the events that happened earlier tonight. I really am deeply sorry," He said with a smile that melted my heart.

I drove home in shock, thinking that if this were true it would eliminate so much financial pressure for me. *This is amazing, or is it too good to be true? Who knows how this stranger will change my life?*

When I arrived home I called Bonnie who was furious with me. I had visions of our friendship and our nights of eating chips and listening to Air Supply dissolving like an Alka Seltzer fizzing out in a cup of water. She slammed the phone down on me for the second time. But I had to tell someone, so I called Garrett and he was as excited as I was. He thought that this guy was incredible and that I was so lucky that my car was getting paid off. He promised he would come over the next day and we would wait together for the phone call to come in.

The next day, he and I were sitting by the phone and sure enough the call came in from Tony's secretary asking for the financial information on my car.

"Wow! Smash! Bang! Crash! What a miracle! What did I do to deserve this?" Garrett shared in the moment and my dear friend was sincerely happy for me.

The following Monday afternoon, Tony called me at the office.

"Is there an area in front of your office where I can land my helicopter to take you to dinner in style?" he asked through a static filled line.

I literally dropped the phone and ran to the front door. I couldn't believe my ears as I flew back to the telephone and stared at the red hold button flashing. *What am I supposed to say?* I was beside myself. My agents didn't know what was going on with me. They watched me frantically losing control, running around the office like a maniac. I certainly didn't have the authority to let him land his helicopter on company grounds. *What should I do? Ask someone stupid.*

"Hi boss, sorry to disturb you, but can I have a minute of your time?" I asked my manager as I knocked on his open door.

"Sure, come on in and have a seat. Are you all right? You look a little pale and disheveled."

"No, yes, I'm all right.Can my friend Tony land his helicopter out in front of our building; he wants to take me out to dinner?"

"Are you kidding me?" he asked, "What is going on with you, Dori? No way! There isn't enough property for him to land a helicopter here!"

"Ok, boss, thanks anyway."

I rushed back and hit the flashing red hold button and apologized for the long time on hold. As my breath and the beat of my heart caught up with each other, I accepted to meet Tony for dinner at his favorite Mexican restaurant. I was a little more calm, but not much. My mind was elsewhere, and I was oblivious to my agents. I couldn't concentrate the rest of the day and left work early to get ready for my dinner date.

Having been in the cosmetic business with mom and having had access to the fashion industry, I always wanted to look my very best. So with that in mind, the winning outfit for that night was my skin-tight black leather pants and a fabulous ivory satin top. I had a very strange feeling this dinner with Tony was about to change my life. *I can't wait!*

During dinner, Tony presented me with an offer that I couldn't refuse.

"Dori, I want to add you to my payroll and give you financial freedom."

As he continued to explain the procedure, I was getting more and more excited and forgot to breathe.

"Fine Tony, no problem," I said, completely trusting him. *This is so exciting. I can't believe this is happening to me!*

"Will you excuse me, Dori, I'll be right back."

"Sure."

As I watched him enter the men's room, I sat there daydreaming and cooing for a few minutes, not knowing what hit me. I would never have another worry for the rest of my life. Tony came back a few minutes later and said,

"Thank you very much, Dori, for accepting my offer." *Thanks, he says.*

"No, thank you so much," I said, hanging on to his every word.

"Effective today, anything you purchase on your credit cards will be paid off every month. All you have to do is sign the credit card receipt as you usually do and add the code 01 next to your signature. Then give the receipt to me, and I will turn it into my company," he explained.

I was stunned; I was going to have an expense-free life! Who knew moving to Dallas would bring me so much happiness and success in such a short time? I pushed my dinner plate away because I couldn't eat another bite.

To look at him, he wasn't my type. He had dirty blonde hair, thin and straggly. He was very tall and lanky. His baggy suit, designed by my girlfriends Polly and Ester, seemed too large and hung loosely on his thin frame. His demeanor was exceptionally low key. I was willing to completely ignore all this, along with his poor choice in restaurants. Chemistry was non-existent between us; however, he did have other good qualities. For instance, he was a great conversationalist with a great sense of humor. When we finished our meal he encouraged me to use my credit card.

"Go ahead, dear, pay the bill. Your new life of financial freedom begins tonight. However, please don't forget to write the code 01 on the receipt and give me the customer copy."

"No problem, Tony." I said and did as he said. He walked me to my car and kissed me goodnight on the cheek and promised to call me the next day. As I drove off I glanced in my rearview mirror and saw him standing there watching me disappear into traffic. *What a kind man.*

I arrived at work the next morning and tried to act as normal as possible. Concentrating on my work was next to impossible and being in a supervisory position demanded a great deal of responsibility that I couldn't seem to handle right then. My agents were asking me all sorts of questions that I wasn't hearing because my mind was thinking at warp speed about my new life and the new man who was making it happen. Suddenly, my strong, independent, capable mind was now, unbeknownst to me, nothing more than a bowl of mush in a blender of confusion. My job was the last thing on my mind, because in all reality (my reality) I no longer had to work for a living.

"Dori, telephone, it's Mr. Stevens." My thoughts were interrupted.

"Hi Tony." my voice rang in a singsong tone.

"Dori, can you meet me at the realtor's office tonight?"

"Of course, what's the address?" I asked excitedly anticipating what was next on the agenda.

I arrived at the real estate office exactly at 6:30pm. Tony approached my car immediately. This felt strangely familiar.

"Dori, I want to purchase a home for us."

"What did you say?" I asked.

"I want to buy a home for us," he said, repeating himself.

"You are the most generous person I have ever met in my whole life! Absolutely!" I said. At this point I had abandoned any practical thinking and reverted to my fantasy world, while *shpilkes* (pins and needles) were setting in even more.

The realtor, Mattie Edwards, took us out looking for homes in the more elite areas of North Dallas. I eagerly jotted down the addresses of the most incredible looking homes. Each home had plush grounds, rolling hills, and the most amazing landscaping. I had never seen such beautiful homes in all of my life. Mattie made some appointments for the following evening. Tony couldn't go because he had other obligations, but told me to pick out the house I wanted and he would see it later.

Afterwards, I met him for dinner to celebrate. I couldn't wait to tell Bonnie all about my new life and how wrong she had been. We spent the evening talking about his life and his parents, who lived in Southern Florida on ten acres of land complete with a runway. I tried to listen as he talked, but my mind was racing a mile a minute thinking that I was going to marry this man. This was a dream come true. The evening came to an end. I, of course charged the bill and gave the receipt to Tony. He gave me a kiss on the cheek as we parted company for the evening.

The following morning I was floating on cloud nine and decided that I needed to take a leave of absence from work since I was about to get married and needed to make all the preparations.

"Take as much time as you need, your job will always be here waiting for you," My boss said, sincerely happy for me.

That evening I went out again with Mattie and toured many properties with prices beginning at $500,000. We looked at several elegant homes which made me feel high on life. I felt like I was on top of the world and everything was mine for the taking. Sleep was something I wasn't getting lately; my poor roommate Marcy couldn't believe the change in my life, or in me. The next morning I telephoned Mom, Jennifer, Bonnie, and Garrett so I could share my extraordinary news. Bonnie didn't answer, so I left a message for her; she never did return my call. But I thought it was her loss and about how wrong she really had been. Perhaps she was just jealous of my suddenly found happiness.

That day I found the home of my dreams, and when I walked into the master bedroom, I cried and demanded that Mattie call Tony immediately and tell him, "This is it!"

I was shocked at my words and the tone of my voice. Tony joined us later to see the home, and he loved it as well.

"Let's go back to your office and draw up the papers," He told her confidently, placing his arm around my waist.

Back at her office Mattie presented me with a signed purchase agreement showing the sales price of almost $700,000.00, followed by bold printed words **PAID IN FULL, IN CASH.** *Yes, Tony Stevens signed it.*

"Living in a material world and I am a material girl."

My heart was pounding, and I could hardly breathe. I tried very hard to take a reality check; however, my thoughts had floated away with the rest of me as this man swept me off my feet.

The following morning Tony wanted me to meet with his secretary to go over some papers while he was working in his office. Mrs. Dawson asked me for some personal information and had me sign a few papers, which I gladly did, and then it dawned on me to question her motives,

"What is this all about?"

"Mr. Stevens has approved you to be added to our payroll." She went on to reassure me that the company would have my car paid off and all my living expenses would be reimbursed.

"I already know all that," I said, feeling patronized by her demeanor.

I brushed it off and left with Tony for a fun-filled night on the town, using my credit cards every step of the way.

It was the following Saturday morning, when Tony called. Immediately after I said hello, he said firmly, "Dori, be ready in one hour, my limo will pick you up!"

I was barely awake that morning, and then suddenly I felt overwhelmed as if I had to gasp for air.

"I'll be ready," I said.

With sweaty palms and a heart rate of 500 beats per minute, I hung up the phone and ran to share the news with Marcy. And she went wild. An hour later the doorbell rang; it was Tony's limo driver.

"Are you ready Ma'am? Mr. Stevens is here waiting for you."

As the driver escorted me to the limo, Tony was seated inside this magnificent limousine vigorously trying to pop the cork on a bottle of champagne. It wasn't the best champagne, but I continued to accept his poor choices in the food and drink departments.

We were off on a buying frenzy like I had never known. We bought everything from clothes to jewels and many things in between. I bought him a designer suit with all the accessories hoping to make him look better than ever, but even a bright blue silk tie could not erase the pale nerdy look that made up his appearance.

"Pretty woman, walking down the street."

I bought everything my heart desired. All I had to do was sign my charge slips with 01 next to my signature and hand them to him. I wanted to buy him anything he wanted, but he insisted that I buy myself things as well, so after a few dress boutiques we were off to Tiffany's for diamond earrings. My credit history was excellent, so Tiffany's opened an account for me within fifteen minutes with an extremely high credit limit. I felt unstoppable.

During dinner I gave Tony all my signed and coded receipts, and he happily took them from me.

"We will pick you up tomorrow around noon, so be ready," he told me as the limo driver took me home.

I ran into my apartment, packages and all, screaming for Marcy. She rushed out of her bedroom to see why I was yelling. When she saw all of my packages her look of shock changed into a look of disappointment. After we exchanged a few words, I noticed that she had become cool towards me.

"I feel like I can't relate to your whirlwind of excitement. It's hard to communicate with you anymore about everyday things. I miss my old friend, Dori," she confessed.

I gave her a big hug and assured her that I would always be there for her whenever she needed me. I didn't know it at the time but this drastic change in my behavior and lifestyle was taking a toll on all of my relationships.

The next day, when the driver pulled up, Marcy seemed a little more excited for me. I felt like a movie star going to a premiere. Tony and I went driving again, and we stopped to visit my friend Garrett. He met us at the door, still in his pajamas. His uptight body language was yelling loudly in disapproval of all that I was doing. I knew he was probably angry with me because I hadn't talked to him in two weeks, and I usually talked to him at least once a day. He reluctantly got into the limo and met Tony. His furrowed brow showed a sense of disgust for Tony, but I ignored it, along with the warning bells that were finally ringing in my head. I knew I wasn't in love with Tony, but I wanted to believe I could grow to love him over the years. But the oddest thing was he never tried to make any sexual advances towards me. Even stranger, I found it to be quite acceptable. After a brief time of small talk, Garrett returned to his house, and we were off and running.

"Honey, Michael Jackson is performing here in Dallas. Would you like to fly over Texas Stadium during the concert and invite your roommate Marcy?" he asked so sweetly.

"I don't know if she'll come, but I'll try."

As usual when I arrived home, I yelled for Marcy and she came running to greet me. As soon as I saw her I babbled on and on about the day, the Michael Jackson concert, then I invited her to join us.

"I'm sorry, I already have dinner plans." She said. Her words were like needles, deflating my happy balloon.

"Marcy, you have to go. It's a private jet, Michael Jackson, and flying over Texas Stadium! Come on! What's wrong with you?"

My voice justified everything, and I convinced her to join us. She softened; then we both grabbed each other's arms, jumped in circles, screaming with excitement. *At last, she will see for herself that my reality was authentic!*

71

"I can finally see why you have changed so much; I'm sorry if I ever doubted you," she said remorsefully.

"It's okay; I would be freaked out too," I said.

We arrived at the airport that evening and Tony was standing there with a huge smile waiting for us.

"This brand new jet is my wedding gift to you," he said and waved his hand in front of the plane that we were about to board. Marcy was shocked by his overwhelming generosity. This time I wasn't scared when the doors of the jet slammed shut behind me.

"Dori, now I can understand your behavior for the last month or so. I feel like a million dollars, too," Marcy said as she sipped her Bloody Mary.

After a few minutes of flying, Tony gave the controls to his co-pilot and joined us.

"Look to your left ladies, you will see Texas Stadium." We obediently looked out. As we turned back to Tony, he had gotten down on his knees in front of me.

"Dori, will you marry me and be my wife?"

"YES, YES and YES, I WILL MARRY YOU!" I screamed, and since Marcy was my witness, it helped to dissolve any doubts that she or I may have had. Even though the plane had landed, I was still floating high on cloud nine.

"Honey, there are newspaper reporters outside near the gate, waiting to interview you. Why don't you go and hide in the pilot's private lounge, so you won't be bombarded by the paparazzi?"

"Okay," I agreed. Marcy and I went to the private lounge and waited. But I was not waiting patiently; I looked around the room, searching for a telephone.

"I have to call my mom, right now!" I was frantic as I dialed her number, my hand shaking like a leaf.

"Dori darling, how are you?" were the only words she could get in, before I began blurting out all the events going on in my life.

"And guess what, Mom, you're not going to believe this, but I'm going to marry him. He already bought us a home in North Dallas!" I said and waited for her response, but silence was all I heard on the other side of the phone.

"Mom, did you hear me?"

"Yes, I'm listening honey. What's his name?" she asked soberly.

"Tony Stevens and he's so wealthy and owns jets and everything!" I jabbered at her.

"Please call Lori and your lady friend the news reporter so she can do a story on my whirlwind romance and my life! She could title it 'Dori Does Dallas'!"

"Okay Dori, I will." She said, I could tell she was smiling for me. She was exasperated by my endless jabbering, but nevertheless, she was supportive, as always.

The driver took the three of us back to the apartment, and we spent the night talking with each other and calling our friends. When I called Jen and woke her up at 2:00am, she was ecstatic and said, "Oh Dori, can I be your maid of honor?"

We all fell asleep around four in the morning. I was the first one up just a few hours later, and I felt numb. I put on a pot of coffee and checked on Marcy who was sound asleep in her bed and then checked on Tony who had fallen asleep in mine, curious why he still hadn't tried anything. While I was having a cup of coffee and a cigarette, the telephone rang. It was a long distance call from mom's friend, the news reporter. She wanted to interview Tony and me for her story.

After I had spent a few minutes on the phone with her, she asked to speak with Tony, who had awakened and was sitting at the table drinking coffee.

"Tony, this is the reporter who wants to do a story on us. She wants to ask you a few questions."

I handed the cordless phone to Tony, and he took it into the other room, passing Marcy on his way. She and I listened by the bedroom door. He told her some basic information about himself and then talked about our wedding.

"I know Streisand is Dori's favorite actress and singer. I was planning on having her perform at our wedding!" Marcy and I looked at each other in shock.

"Marcy, I feel like I'm going to either throw up or pass out!" I could barely hold back the tears of excitement and joy that I felt. After he hung up, I began sobbing tears of joy.

The following week was filled with so much activity that my feet never touched the ground. We went looking for an engagement ring and checked out different hotels for our wedding. Lori, my levelheaded sister, was suspicious and wanted to fly out and meet the man who had swept me off my feet. We flew her in for a long weekend to get to know Tony. As soon as I saw her beautiful face, I immediately got out of the limo; we hugged and kissed. I was so excited she had come to meet my fiancé.

As we entered the car, I proudly made the introductions. Lori's mouth fell open in shock when she saw Tony. She looked at me in utter disbelief; Tony was definitely not the tall, dark, and handsome man that I had always dreamt of marrying. All weekend I ignored her negative comments and the sour look on her face and just enjoyed sharing my happiness with my sister. At the end of our weekend we said goodbye at the airport, and all Lori could do was shake her head back and forth. With tears running down her cheeks, she waved good-bye.

I pushed any negative feelings about Tony and the entire situation to the back of my mind. After all, I had a wedding to plan. I could sense that Marcy was feeling uneasy as well. She told me, "I can't take this anymore! I'm even taking some medication to calm myself down. Dori, maybe you would like some?"

However, there was no talking to me at this point; I was living in my own fantasy world. I realized that I had not talked with any of my good friends in a long time, but dismissed it as not having anything in common with them anymore. I was with Tony constantly. I had lost all concept of reality as we prepared to decorate our new home and plan for the wedding. I was charging up a storm and had depleted my savings, but none of that worried me. In my eyes, Tony was for real and all the material things that I owned were real as well. I knew I was going to be reimbursed from his company for every cent, so I had nothing to worry about.

Through an invitation from Garrett, I decided to attend the Republican National Convention where both former President Gerald Ford and Mr. Ross Perot would be in attendance. I went, hoping I would be able to meet Mr. Perot and get his advice on starting my own business. I felt unstoppable, and nothing or no one could get in my way. I went dressed to kill and walked through security like I was a member of the Republican Party. As I stood in the reception line to meet the former President and his wife, I was nervous, not knowing what to say. I took my cues from the people around me and simply repeated what the others had said.

"Your speech was wonderful," I said as I shook the dignitary's hand.

Tony couldn't go with me because of some pressing business so he came over that night to see how it went. He brought his briefcase with him and we sat and chatted, then he excused himself and headed for the restroom. I thought about the fact that I hadn't been reimbursed for anything yet and then out of curiosity I took a peek in his briefcase. To my amazement it was loaded with stacks and stacks of crisp, new one hundred dollar bills. I couldn't believe my eyes, and I began to question things. But, as soon as he reappeared from the bathroom, those thoughts flew out of my mind. I had asked him why I hadn't been reimbursed for anything yet, and he brushed it off saying that it takes time to get the accounts in order.

"You know, I want you to meet my parents. What about tomorrow?"

"Sure I want to meet them; they're going to be my parents, too." I said sincerely.

"I'll be by at eleven-thirty to pick you up." He gave me a long kiss good night and said, "I love you."

I leaned against the door and sighed. *I'm the luckiest girl in the world.*

"Some boys try and some boys lie."

The next morning, Tony arrived right on time; however, he arrived in his own car, the one I hadn't seen since we met in the parking lot of the mall.

"I hope you don't mind, Dori, but we have to drive my car instead of the limo; my parents are very conservative."

"No problem, honey. Oh, I forgot to tell you that the reporter called yesterday. She was having trouble confirming the information you gave her, but I told her to do a little more checking."

As we drove I recalled that his parents lived on an estate in Southern Florida, but we hadn't left Dallas yet. Suddenly, he made a fast right into an old looking subdivision and pulled into the driveway of a modest red brick ranch home. I was a little surprised and confused as the old nervousness began creeping its way back into my head and my stomach. We walked into the humble home and his dad met us at the door.

"Hi Mr. Stevens, I'm Dori, Tony's fiancé," I said, extending my hand to him.

I wonder why Tony hasn't introduced me. He shook my hand and forced a smile on his solemn looking face.

"Nice to meet you, dear. Please come in and have a seat," he said in a soft, depressing voice.

The musty air was thick with tension; I looked at Tony who just rolled his eyes. His dad sat down in his easy chair facing us on the broken down sofa. Then with a sigh, his dad got up and began pacing the room, stopping in front of me.

"First of all, my dear, my name is not Mr. Stevens. I'm Bill Wilson. My son, who is sitting next to you with his tail between his legs, is not Tony Stevens, but Thomas Wilson. You see, dear, he is a very sick young man."

I was afraid to look at Tony for fear he would be nodding his head in agreement with his father's words, which were like ice picks stabbing at my heart and sending chills down my spine.

"My son is out on parole for conning women. He has been in and out of prison over the past several years and will probably go back to prison if you decide to press charges."

His words were cold, dry, and seemed rehearsed, as if he had used them before.

"Tom had to be home today because his parole officer was paying him a visit." He continued, but his words became distant echoes, like a lost ship calling out to a lighthouse in a dense fog. I felt the slap of reality hit me like a car crash. I had a hard time catching my breath, and for the very first time in my life I was speechless.

For a moment in time, I felt like Cinderella and now it was midnight, where my existence, turned into rags, pumpkins, and a wart covered toad. My life was a charade and I was the last to know. A disaster is an understatement, as I mentally counted all of my financial losses. For the last few weeks I had allowed fantasies, wishes, and a false sense of security take over my entire life. I had replaced my true life with a false one and, in turn, lost my job and allowed my wonderfully loyal friends to fall by the wayside. I had never in all of my life felt so disgusted with myself or ashamed of who I was.

"Can you help me in any way?" I asked finally breaking my silence.

"I wish I could dear, but this has been going on with my son for years. You, along with many other young women, have become his victim."

His words were sympathetic and tears welled in his eyes at my anguish. I tried to stay strong, but panic came fast and furious.

"My wife is on her deathbed, and that's where my heart and concerns are right now."

The doorbell rang, breaking the utter silence in the room. It was the parole officer. Bill introduced me and the officer shook my hand, holding it as if to reassure me. He turned to Tony and asked him a few questions about his whereabouts for the past three weeks. Tony admitted he had done it again, which led me to another breakdown. My shoulders were bopping as if they were loaded with Energizer batteries and my eyes were flooded with tears. I was hysterical when I asked the officer, "Would you please drive me home now?"

"Of course, I will," he quickly responded. *Why me? I just want to die!*

I could not look at Tony's ugly and demented face, nor say his name. As I entered the car, I was still crying uncontrollably. The officer handed me some tissues and tried to calm me down.

"Calm down?" I screamed, my nose running like a faucet in full force. "How can I calm down? My life has been destroyed in just a few short weeks!"

"I will try and help you, Dori, as much as I can," he said, trying to comfort me.

"How could he do this to me? Why did he do this to me?" I was simply begging for an answer.

"His plan of action is always the same. He has conned women all over Dallas. He has huge connections from the airlines to real estate companies. He uses other people's planes, cars, and credit cards. Dori, you need to realize that you are the fifth woman he has conned in the last six months. The other four victims have come forward. The FBI thinks he has a tie to a drug ring and they want him bad. Dori, you must press charges. If he is found guilty, you may have a chance to receive restitution," he assured me as he drove.

The officer dropped me off at my apartment, and I knew I was lucky that I hadn't been physically hurt. But I also knew that I had a long road of financial recovery ahead of me. But most of all, I needed to recover mentally and emotionally. When I got in the door of my apartment, I went straight to my bedroom, curled up in my bed, and cried myself to sleep.

A few days later, the parole officer arranged for me to meet with the four other women who were also Tony's victims. They insisted I press charges, and I agreed wholeheartedly. About a week later I heard he had been arrested, which was the good news. However, as time went on, he pled guilty to all the charges against him, meaning no restitution for any of us, which of course was the bad news. I felt so scared and alone and once again my future was in jeopardy. With seventy-five cents in my wallet, I promised myself not to look back and to begin the process of healing and rebuilding my life.

Marcy had decided to move out, for which I couldn't blame her.

"I have to go. I'm about to lose my job. I can't sleep, eat, or concentrate. I'm so sorry this didn't work out, but now I have to think about me," Marcy said remorsefully.

We remained friendly, but I never heard from Bonnie again. The only friendship that lasted was with Garrett. I kept in touch with Jennifer and thank G-d she was still my friend. I knew that the miles between us served as a protective barrier that kept our friendship from becoming tarnished by the event.

Mom and Lori loaned me some money to pay my rent and to help me get back on my feet. I quickly found a new roommate. This was my first step to getting back on my feet financially. I called all of my creditors and set up payment arrangements. After talking with them and assessing the damage I had done, I felt defeated. While my credit was important to me, I knew there was no way I could get out from under all of this debt alone; I felt I had no other choice than to file for bankruptcy in the amount of $30,000.00. I was foolishly suffering from financial setback at the hands of a con man.

The following week, after interviewing with a few different travel agencies, I found a nice sales position with a small travel agency in Dallas called Airline Travel. The owners and their staff were very good to me. I was in outside sales handling corporate travel arrangements, which gave me a lot of freedom. I had to be at the office every morning by 8:30am, just like the other employees. My new boss gave me structure, which is what I needed. Having order back in my life helped me jumpstart the healing process.

CHAPTER FIVE

"Your Heart Will Lead You Home"

Kenny Loggins

It was early February 1985; it had taken me about a year to get back on my feet, and I felt stronger than ever. The weather in Dallas was sunny and a gorgeous 55 degrees. During this time of healing I was able to reconnect with my mother and sister. The telephone became my best friend as I listened to their words of encouragement. I still asked Mom the same question and she would always give me the same answer, only she'd change it to my current age.

"When is it going to happen?" I would ask and then add, "Please don't say, 'Dori darling you are only thirty years old'."

She would say it anyway. But it was a reassurance of something familiar. I began to miss my family,

Jennifer, and my roots. The last time I talked with Jennifer, she was heartbroken over some guy named Sam. She suggested I come back home to Detroit for a visit to meet Sam's friend Marvin. It had been almost a year since my experience with Tony so I thought going home for a visit might not be a bad idea.

The following Friday, I flew back to Detroit and stayed with Mom. We had a great time talking and I felt very loved and supported by her. Lori was glad to see me as well and both of them were too kind to say 'I told you so' in regards to Tony. It was as if none of it had ever happened, and our relationship was stronger than ever.

Early Saturday morning, the phone rang,

"Hi Dori. You're finally home. Is it ok if I come over right now, I can't wait to see you?" Jen said excitedly.

"Of course Jen. I can't wait to see you either, now hurry!" I demanded and hung up the phone.

Maybe a half an hour later, I heard the front door open with a bang and a scream from Jen,

"Hi Dori, I'm here! Where are you?" her voice echoing through the house.

I quickly ran to welcome my friend and together we screamed and embraced each other like never before. We grabbed a glass of ice water, our cigarettes, and went outside to talk in private.

I missed hearing Jen's New York accent, seeing her beautiful green eyes, and feeling our heart-felt friendship. Since our college days, she kept her long blond hair straight as can be and she still battled with her weight. She reminded me of Bette Midler because of her bubbly personality. She was everyone's friend as long as they paid attention to her. Her heart is huge and she is the best listener in the world.

In her late 20's, Jen's family had moved out of state and they left Jennifer all alone and in charge of their movers. She was so overwhelmed by the unwanted responsibility, she called me instead.

"I can't handle it, Dori. Will you come over and supervise?"

"I'll be right over." I said without hesitation. With her parents and my living out of state, Jen was alone here in Detroit, adopting everyone else's family. With me in Dallas and Jen here, the telephone was our only means for keeping in touch. However, it was a weak way to nurture a friendship as close as ours.

"How are you? You look great! I missed you as much as I miss my family. You know you're like a sister to me," Jen said sweetly.

"You too honey. What's happening with you and how's work going?"

"Fine, fine, and fine." She said, in her typical non-emotional words. "Well, you know my friend Sam Gold; he has been so aloof lately, acting as if I don't exist. So I thought the four of us could go out for dinner and dancing tonight."

"Hold it right there, Jen. Who's the fourth person?" I questioned.

"Don't worry, Dori, he's a nice guy and a friend of mine and Sam's. His name is Marvin Silverstein, and he wants to meet you. I think you'll like him."

Fun, that sounds good! Who knew?

"What's even better, I can be with Sam," she said.

"This won't fix anything with you and Sam," I told her.

"Maybe it won't, maybe it will. I can hope can't I?" she responded.

"Ok, I'm game! I hope we are going to meet them somewhere because I don't want a date picking me up at my mommy's house." We both laughed.

We met the guys for dinner, and Sam seemed nice and very personable. Jennifer was smiling so I assume her plan was working. Marv was very nice too, about 5'10" with a full head of dark hair and thick mustache. He seemed to have a fun-loving personality. He kept asking me questions like, "What's so great about Dallas? Why have you been away so long?"

He told me little bits and pieces about himself during the evening.

"I work in the family beauty supply business with my dad, and I love it. I have an older brother and a younger sister. And I have been married twice before."

"That's funny; my ex-husband was married twice before he married me." I added.

All in all, the night went well, but I was flying back to Dallas the next day and there was nothing else to pursue.

First thing Sunday morning, Marv called.

"I had a wonderful time last night. Dori, I wish you weren't going back so soon."

"Marv, you can call me anytime. I promise to be back for another visit real soon. It's no big deal for me to fly home. I'm in the travel business, remember?" We said our goodbyes and Jennifer drove me to the airport, and an element of sadness came right along with us.

As Jennifer popped the trunk, I grabbed my luggage and said, "I love you Jen! Keep me posted on Sam, Okay?"

"I will. Love you too," Jen replied.

"I will miss you even more. Bye-bye," I said, quickly walking away from the car.

"Torn between two worlds."

By Monday, I was back at work. My trip back home to Detroit was bittersweet. I loved Dallas, but at the same time, after seeing my family and Jennifer, I felt like I was missing something. But having just rebuilt my life, I didn't want to mess things up again.

Ever since I got back to Dallas, the telephone began ringing off the hook; it was Marv.

"I had such a good time with you, Dori! I can't stop thinking about you! Let me come out to see you and we can get to know each other better," he demanded.

"I don't know. A long distance relationship will never work." With his persistence, I agreed.

In early April, I nervously picked him up at the Dallas/Fort Worth airport.

"Hi Dori, it's so good to see you! I missed you," he whispered in my ear, as we embraced.

After I took him back to my apartment and he got settled, I made some ice tea and, sitting on my sofa, he began his nonstop persuasion; listing all the reasons I should move back home.

"Dori, please move home. You're right; long distance relationships don't work. I've never met anyone like you and I want to be with you."

"No, Marvin, I can't! I refuse to give up the life I've built here in Dallas. I can't afford to start over and screw up again."

Marv appeared to understand for the moment and didn't bring it up again all weekend. We had a wonderful few days together and when he left on

Sunday, I felt like part of my roots went with him. He called immediately when he got home.

"I miss you, Dori; come to Detroit for a two day visit just with me," he asked sweetly. I agreed and a couple of weeks later I was back in Detroit.

I had an opportunity to see how Marv lived. He drove a bright yellow Ford Fiesta, nothing the average 35-year-old man would drive, and he lived in the poorer part of town. It seems that his father completely controlled his life, including where he lived and what he drove. Ignoring all this, I happily discovered I now had feelings for Marv and I felt sorry for him too. *I will help him and show him how to be his own man.*

"Dori, please move back to Detroit and live with me." I kissed him goodbye and boarded the plane back to Dallas and got right back into the swing of things. Though his words were sincere, I knew I couldn't move back to Detroit just for the sake of relocating.

My career was rewarding and moving steadily forward. I built up a client base and my commissions were increasing. I loved my new boss and my friendship with Garrett was stronger than ever. My attraction for Marv was growing more and more with each telephone call.

Now, at the age of thirty-something, I realized my maternal instincts were tugging at me and my biological clock was ticking faster than ever. Oh, I wanted to hold a baby in my arms, cuddle him, sit in a white rocking chair and watch him coo. I needed to be a mommy so bad, and I couldn't wait much longer to have my son. I began feeling confused because of Marv's continued pursuit. He knew I wasn't coming back to Detroit without some kind of plan.

"Dori, I want to marry you and have children."

I told him that I would think about it and make a decision.

I really needed to see Jennifer so I invited her for a visit. On August 2, 1985, it was a frightening drive to the airport. I could hardly see the white lines on the road due to the awful thunderstorm and the dense fog. As soon as I arrived, I checked the monitors for arrivals and most of them flashed delayed. I had left her itinerary in the car so I didn't know the flight number. Suddenly, a deep male voice came over the public address system:

"There's been a tragic accident, Delta flight 191 has gone down. We are unaware of the severity and will keep you posted. Please remain calm. A representative will be out to see you momentarily."

Since I didn't have her flight number I began to panic, thinking her plane had crashed. I felt hopeless and helpless at the same time as I began to cry uncontrollably. I ran back to the monitors and checked all the other incoming flights on Delta and they all flashed delayed too.

Oh my G-d, Jen must be scared out of her mind. I wish I was there to squeeze her hand and tell her everything will be alright.

A man was walking by, and I yelled.

"Sir, do you know if that's the flight from Detroit?" he just looked at me like I was nuts and he kept walking.

My best friend is dead! I can't lose her - she's like a sister to me. Dear G-d, please bring Jennifer to me. I'll take care of her, just let her be safe. I checked my watch; it had been twenty minutes since I had heard anything. I walked over to the monitors and carefully read the flight information again, "LANDED" flashing in green. And within minutes, I saw her walk through the doors, and I ran to hug her. Thank G-d she wasn't on the downed plane after all. As usual, Jen made light of the whole thing.

"What's wrong with you, Dori? My plane was just circling and couldn't land because of bad weather."

"I know, just give me another hug. I love you so much." I said relieved. *Thank you, G-d.*

Unbeknownst to her, Delta flight 191 from Ft Lauderdale had crashed. One hundred and thirty five people were killed in the disaster.

The month of August is steamy hot in Dallas. At one point during our visit we spent the day at the pool with Garrett. Jennifer was so hot, she jumped into his pool, clothes and all. It was good to see her laughing and smiling again because she was still having a hard time in her relationship with Sam. It was going nowhere fast because his feelings focused on just being friends and nothing more. Her emotions were out of control, which led to a lot of tears, something very rare for her to express.

"Please move home, Dori, I need you—everyone needs you, whether you end up with Marvin or not," she said, in all sincerity.

"I'll think about it, okay?" I said.

"It's a deal," she responded.

"The ones who care
They all will be waiting there."

After Jennifer's visit I did some serious thinking and took a hard look at the new life I had built. Throughout the past thirty years, with my dad leaving, having a failed marriage, and then the horrific nightmare of "Tony the Con Man", I found that starting over had become a way of life for me. My world was stable, just the way I liked it. But there was this overshadowing feeling that something or someone was missing from it. I was miles away from my Detroit roots and missing all of the life changing moments happening to Mom, Lori, and Jennifer. The following evening I had a long talk with Marv and accepted his marriage proposal on one condition.

"Marv can we please live together first, before we get married?" I asked.

He reluctantly agreed; after all we didn't really know each other that well, and I wanted to take this relationship slowly. He promised to find us an apartment so I could move in directly when I arrived from Dallas.

I was set to leave in three weeks, which at the time, felt like an eternity. I wrote out my resignation letter, still slightly uncertain of my actions. My boss and co-workers gave me a wonderful going away party with champagne and all the extras.

The hardest part was saying farewell to Garrett. We had become such good friends, much like the two main characters on the television show *Will and Grace*. After I broke the news to him, he was less than thrilled about it, but the next day he called me at the office.

"Dori, I have two tickets to Los Angeles. Go home and pack your things, we are leaving tonight!" Garrett said, wanting one last weekend together before I left for good. He had become my best male girlfriend, and we stayed at the beautiful Beverly Hills Hotel for the entire weekend. We reminisced about the good times and he promised to come to my wedding.

"Are you sure this time? Your track record isn't that great. Don't you think you're moving too fast?" he asked carefully.

"Thank you, my friend, for caring so much." I said. I knew then, going home was the right thing for me to do.

In September, I was back home in Detroit. Marv took care of everything; he had already rented an apartment for us. I felt very nervous about the whole thing, especially after the events of the last year. But as we talked and shared our hopes and dreams, we agreed to stay in the apartment for one year and then, after we were married, we'd look for a house and begin our family.

I applied for a job right away at a travel agency selling corporate travel once again. They wanted me to start the following Monday. Marv was not as receptive about my new job as I hoped he'd be, and I wasn't sure why. When I tried to talk with him about it, he was hesitant and then told me he wasn't sure he wanted me to work outside the home. I chose to ignore his uncertainty and began my new job, which I enjoyed immensely. We had been living together for three short weeks when he began pressuring me to plan our wedding.

"Let's set a date; we can't live like this forever! I love you, Dori, and that's all that matters," he kept insisting.

"This is way to soon; we don't even know each other. I thought waiting at least one year was understood?"

"I want to start a family! I'm not getting any younger. We have so much to do and I can't wait that long."

"This is crazy! I have just been through so much. I want this wonderful life, too. Won't you wait just a little longer?"

"No, honey, I want you to be my wife and the mother of my children." I felt scared and trapped but I did love him. *He just paid all my expenses to move back home, how can I back out now?* I was thirty-one years old and didn't have much time left. And being a mommy had become very important to me.

We set a date for May of 1986, the following spring. Jennifer was ecstatic, and mom offered to help me find a place for the wedding. All the support just reconfirmed that I was doing the right thing. Jennifer, of course, was in the middle of everything, and she was so excited you would think it was her wedding. She was going to be my bridesmaid, honoring me as she always had. As the wedding day approached, my nerves were in shambles. Mom and I found a beautiful restaurant, decorated in pinks and plums, and the head chef was well known for his great entrees. The ambiance was perfectly romantic for our wedding. We had decided on a fancy cocktail party with a light dinner for our families and closest friends. Rabbi Stein agreed to conduct the ceremony at the restaurant. Everything was falling into place.

Marv and I scheduled the standard meeting with the rabbi prior to our nuptials. During our meeting, my fiancé left for the restroom. The rabbi said in a stern tone, "Dori, there should have been a helicopter at your first wedding to take you away from that man, whatever his name was."

"I know and thank G-d, I got out. Thank you, Rabbi." I walked around his desk and gave him a warm bear hug.

"Dori, are you sure this man is right for you?" he asked skeptically.

"Oh yes, Rabbi. We're going to look for a house and start a family right away."

"You know dear, I always thought you would be my daughter-in-law, one day." *Wow, was he talking to me?*

"I didn't know you felt that way," I said shyly.

"I would have been honored, and Marvin is a lucky man. Alright, see you under the *chupa* (canopy) at your wedding. If you ever need me, you know where to find me."

"Thank you, Rabbi." I said sincerely.

Marv walked back in and the Rabbi said to him, "Please take care of her."

"I promise I will," he answered with enthusiasm. Rabbi Stein and I always had a special relationship, and I hoped he would always be a part of my life.

CHAPTER SIX

"Somewhere"

Barbra Streisand

The wedding was perfect. I wore a beautiful ivory 1920's-style wedding gown with a matching hat and a veil. Jennifer, Mom, and Lori looked beautiful in their ivory knee-length dresses as well. Jen was in her own little world, sitting next to Sam during dinner. Later that evening I noticed Marv and Jen posing for a picture and glancing into each other's eyes. *I know Jen thinks this is her wedding!* Garrett flew in from Dallas, and I was so happy to see him.

During the reception, I was able to have a few private moments with my sister, Lori. She was struggling in her marriage and had already filed for divorce. Lori never told me anything, and my living out of state hadn't helped. Since she was closed mouth about her private life, this was a total shock. I felt very sad for her because her marriage was breaking up and this reconfirmed why I needed to be back home. By far the worse part was she shut me out of her life. But maybe it was because I was so caught up in my own world. It felt great to be home, and I was determined to be there for her and give her the love and support that she had given me for so many years.

We had a wonderful honeymoon on a Caribbean cruise. After returning home, we went back to our jobs. My husband was obviously disturbed about my working outside the home and voiced his opinion on several occasions.

"Dori, you don't have to work anymore. I want you to stay home; we can afford it."

"Honey, I love my career, that's all I know. What will I do everyday? I'm not into going out to lunch with the girls. If I don't work, I'll just be bored and get fat."

"We can start our family, look for a house and work on getting pregnant. How does that sound?" he asked excitedly. The same conversation went back and forth for a while until I agreed to quit my job because having children was one of the reasons I married him.

After about a month of sleeping in, having lunch with my girlfriends and getting my nails done, I was not only bored, but I had gained weight as well. I looked in the mirror and realized that instead of business suits and pumps, my daily attire had become running shoes and sweats. I was becoming a frumpy housewife, and I didn't like the reflection.

I longed to do something constructive with my time. I decided to go to real estate school and get my license. He seemed to like this idea because he thought it would fizzle out quickly. Middletown Real Estate Training in Southfield, Michigan offered a five-week crash course, so I signed up and started the classes the following week. When I wasn't in class, I was home studying. This course required a lot of reading and homework. My husband made it difficult when he was home by interrupting me and refusing to let me study. I often had to beg him to leave me alone and give me the time to study. I warned him that if I failed, I would just take it again until I passed. He finally got the message and let me be.

One evening we decided to use some of the money that we received from our wedding to purchase a stereo. Years ago he had had a system which his father took from him telling him it was repayment for all the things that he had done for his son. This was so hard for me to believe; that a parent would do something like this. Their relationship continued, but I knew there would be obstacles in the days to come. My husband's life had been enmeshed with his fathers, and I intended to help him fix it.

While we were looking around, he said with concern,

"Dori, we're going to have to talk to my mom and dad about giving us a down payment on a house."

"No problem, honey. If they won't give us the money, we can offer to pay them back. Your dad cannot run our lives, and I'd rather ask for a loan; then hopefully he won't want to control our every move. Okay, honey?" He agreed.

A couple of days later, we invited his parents over to see our new entertainment center. We both felt this would be an opportune time to ask for the money and let them know we are planning to start our family.

"Dad, my wife and I want to start a family and we need to start looking for a house. There's only one problem, we need help with the down payment," he said nervously.

"What did you say? You're still crazy son! Your mother and I are still living in this old house and if you think you are going to have a new home before we do, you have another thing coming! I'm shocked and so is your mother! If you are going to do this, you will be kicked out of the family business and be completely out on your own!" He spoke in a cold, stern voice.

His mother was speechless and I was dumfounded. As they argued back and forth, it was a rude awakening for me to see this kind of control his father had over him and his life.

"And you, young lady, have to sell your car. No one in this family drives a brand new car, ever," my father-in-law said in a daunting voice as he pointed a demeaning finger at me.

I was driving my two-year-old Pontiac Fiero at the time. I couldn't believe he had said this to me and how spineless my husband was in front of his father. Abruptly, his parents walked out; my mother-in-law never said a word. Marv looked at me with tears in his eyes. *Oh my G-d, I had no idea his dad had this much power over him.*

"Honey, we don't need your dad. Why don't you think about getting your own job away from your father's business? If you accomplish that, we can be free to build our life together on our own," I offered, trying to be encouraging and supportive. But for some reason he disregarded everything I had said.

"I have to stay working for him; I don't know how to do anything else!" Marv finally said and broke the silence.

I realized then and there that we couldn't start a family. I could not bring a child into such a controlling environment.

We were married only three months when I finished real estate training and passed my state boards with flying colors. This was a boost to my self-esteem; now instead of dreaming of having children with Marv, I decided to pour myself into my new real estate career.

One afternoon while I was typing my résumé, I received a call from my husband who was clearly upset and couldn't talk straight.

"Slow down honey, I can hardly understand you."

"I said, "My father thinks that I'm stealing from the business."

"Why?" I stopped typing and sighed, rolling my eyes at their relationship.

"My brother goes to the same bank we use and he received our statement by accident. Anyway he opened the statement which had the cancelled check from the electronics store where we bought our stereo and he went ballistic and called my dad!" Marv said frantically crying.

"Marv, please honey, calm down. We bought that with our wedding money," I defended.

"I've got to go, I'll be home soon," he said.

I put the phone down, thinking that this incident was the beginning of the end of our marriage. I had married Marvin, not his father. But clearly his dad had come with the vows. I felt invaded and knew I couldn't live like this.

I had to get my mind off of it and called mom to find out how she had been doing. Due to the recession of the early eighties, mom's business had gone under and she was talking about moving out of state; she wanted to travel a little and then settle somewhere warmer. Lori was doing alright; she still didn't talk about the downfall of her marriage, but her new puppy, a golden retriever named Rockie, had lifted her spirits.

In 1987, I had found a job with a major real estate company. It had a remarkable training program for new realtors. They took good care of their agents and prepared me in every way for my new career. At this time, things were getting progressively worse at home. Marv was becoming extremely possessive of me, not even wanting me to talk on the phone with Lori, Jennifer, or my mom. He would call my office, sometimes ten times a day to check and see when I would be home. This had become an inconvenient and embarrassing situation. I told the receptionist to tell him I was out with a client.

One rainy evening, Lori came over to visit us. She had found a wet stray Calico kitten outside the apartment. She brought this helpless animal in and I immediately began cuddling it.

"Who does that thing belong to?" Marv asked.

"I found her outside, meowing." Lori said.

"Sure you did. You two girls planned the whole thing. You set me up and you're trying to frame me." Lori and I looked at each other in shock and we refused to acknowledge his ridiculous accusations. I decided to keep her and name her, Samantha.

I didn't want another divorce. All I wanted to do was save my marriage and start a family. However, I knew this was never going to happen. I was thirty-three years old and the idea of having a child was looking bleaker by the day. So I called the one person I thought could really help us, Rabbi Stein.

I included my in-laws in our first session, which turned into a huge disaster. My father-in-law wouldn't listen to anything the rabbi said, my mother-in-law said very little, and Marv stayed as quiet as a mouse. The rabbi looked at me with eyes of compassion, and I nodded in agreement. We both knew that I was in a tough situation once again, and a second meeting as a family wasn't an option.

"Hold my hand and we're half way there."

Marv and I decided to go through marriage counseling, as we didn't want to give up on us. The female counselor, Carol, recommended we meet every Tuesday at 4:00pm. We liked her and began making some progress with each session. There were some ugly moments, which included screaming and yelling. However, Carol immediately brought us under control. After four weeks of therapy, I started to see a positive change in his behavior and the tension at home began to ease up.

"I think we have a chance, Honey. I see how hard you are trying. It makes a difference when you treat me like your wife instead of a material posses-sion," I lovingly told him.

"I feel, Honey, we're having a breakthrough and I want our marriage to work," Marv responded lovingly.

"Me too and I can't wait until we see Carol again!" I said.

My husband was really making a strong effort; he was not calling ten times a day at the office, and he was treating me with love and respect. I was thrilled about the potentially positive outcome of my marriage. In my mind I thought I could fix things, especially if I could share my strength and support with him and help him leave the family business and cut his father's tight strings.

Marv and I walked into our next Tuesday session holding hands. Carol was taken aback as she asked, "What has happened here?"

"Go ahead, Honey; tell her about the breakthrough we've had improving our communication as husband and wife. How you're not calling me every 30 minutes at the office, our loving talks about staying together, and starting a family." I urged him. However, nothing came out of his mouth as if I were imagining all the positive changes that had taken place between us. *I feel like such a fool. Maybe he's just playing games? But marriage is not a game, and I'm out of here.* He looked at me blankly as if he had nothing to say. I was dumbfounded by his lack of response and I went berserk.

"That's it! I'm finished trying. I'm done with therapy, and you and I are over! What a waste of time this has been," I said through tears of frustration, while storming out of Carol's office.

We had been married for a year and a half when I had to find another divorce attorney. I moved out the following Sunday after Marv left for bowling. The movers showed up right on time, and I quickly stuffed my personal things in garbage bags. I was so angry and felt so empty inside that I wanted him to come home and feel the same way I did. Feeling hurt by his denial in therapy, and all thoughts of saving my second failed marriage were dead. *One thing is for sure, I will never marry again. Goodbye Marvin, have a nice life!*

Jennifer's and my mutual friend offered her living room couch as a temporary place for me to live. I felt so horrible leaving my cat Samantha, but I would come back for her as soon as I could.

The following week, the reality of a commission-only income hit me. I planned on leaving my new career for a steady paycheck, when my boss offered me a draw against commission, which enabled me to receive a check on the first of every month, guaranteed. This was unheard of in the real estate industry, but I felt so grateful; I had a job that now offered me a regular income and some sort of permanence, which was a new experience for me.

During my separation from Marv, Jennifer kept in close contact with me. She called every day to make sure I was alright. She showed compassion and offered to help me find a new apartment when I was ready.

"I love you, Dori; don't worry you'll be fine!"

"Thanks, Jen. I love you too!" Her love and support meant everything to me.

However, what I didn't know was that she had been staying in touch with Marv as well. One evening I was having dinner with Marv who wanted to discuss working things out to avoid the divorce. The first thing I did was check on my cat Samantha. Her food dish was dried up and her water bowl was empty. I knew I was taking her with me that night. After dinner, we spent hours talking about our problems. He apologized for his childlike behavior at the therapist's office, and pleaded with me not to go through with the divorce. I felt confused for a quick moment until he blurted out, "Jennifer is not your friend!"

"What are you talking about?" I asked him, dropping my fork.

He went on to tell me that she had been informing him of every detail of my life.

"You are a liar! Prove it," I said, standing and almost knocking over the chair. Marv proceeded to give me a play-by-play itinerary of where I had been during this past weekend, including a visit with my sister. Marv was exactly right. He would have no way of knowing what I was doing or where I was going, but Jennifer knew everything. I sat back down in shock, shaking my head at my best friend's behavior. I knew he wasn't lying to me. I was betrayed, hurt and angry. I grabbed the nearest phone and hastily dialed Jennifer's number, while Marv sheepishly watched me. I didn't realize it was 3:00am and of course she was sleeping, but I didn't care.

"Jennifer, your sick game is over. I'm finished with you. You're a liar and a phony. I didn't know Marv was your best friend too! I never want to speak to you again, ever!"

I slammed the phone down, picked up my cat and stormed out the door. I drove to Lori's house and rang her doorbell.

"I'm so sorry to wake you like this, can I move in?" I asked, while tears fell on to my cat who was cuddled in my arms. Lori pulled me in, gave me a hug, and I moved in that following weekend.

It was the day of the divorce hearing on a beautiful Michigan spring morning. I was sipping my morning coffee and thinking that in a matter of hours I would once again be a free woman. I was scheduled to be in court at ten, and I felt nervous, sad and peaceful all at the same time. I felt nervous because I was going through another divorce, sad because I wasn't going to start having my babies and peaceful because I was about to be free from this dysfunctional family. I was startled from my thoughts by the telephone.

"Hi Dori, guess who? Can I drive you to the courthouse?" Marv asked.

"This is a very hard day for me, please let me pick you up," he added in a whining voice.

I declined, feeling shaky inside, but he was persistent until I gave in to him. I didn't think riding with him would do any harm.

"We'll find a way of forgiving."

When he arrived, he held out a dozen long stem red roses with a card attached. I looked at the card; it was a picture of a dog lying in the doghouse with his head sticking out. Marv scribbled on it, "Please don't divorce me today, I Love You!"

I sighed, knowing that I should never have said yes to his ride, but I resolved to remain strong. I had to ignore his outbursts and personal pity parties. Yet, during the entire thirty minute drive all he did was beg and plead with me not to go through with the divorce. I kept telling myself to stay strong and don't give in.

He parked the car far from the main entrance of the courthouse, which gave him more time to talk me out of this. I felt so anxious that I began sweating as we waited for my attorney who was representing both of us. *I feel so bad, what should I do? Here I go again, feeling sorry for him.*

"Here comes our attorney, Marvin," I said as he lowered his head in sadness. *Oh my G-d, I can't do this! What's wrong with me? Maybe Marv and I have a chance? I want to have a baby. I already have one failed marriage.* Suddenly his arrival felt like time came to a screeching halt and I was making a huge mistake.

"Are you ready, Dori?" Gary asked.

"Marv got to me. After all I've been through I guess I still need more time. No, I'm not ready and I'm sorry I wasted your time."

Gary left in a huff; however, my husband was relieved which he expressed in a gigantic hug. When

Marv dropped me off at home, I stood at the front door not knowing what had happened and then I realized he had manipulated me. I stood up straight, sighed, and walked into the house to call my attorney. He informed me that it would be three months before we could schedule another court date.

During those three months, Marv called constantly, until I finally told him to stop calling and our marriage was over. Three months later we were divorced. Once again, I felt sorry for him, just like when we first met. I realized while we were standing in front of the judge that I always felt sorry for the men in my life, starting with my father who was a very needy person. My attraction to these men was their need for me. In my mind, I could fix everything and help or change them so their life would be better. This is what my parents taught me my entire childhood. They needed me to fix things based on their weaknesses. Mom thought I could make her life better and so did my dad. Unbeknownst to me, this was causing me to make the wrong choices in my life because now I too was weak. After our day in court, Marv and I parted amicably.

With 2 failed marriages behind me, I had developed an allergy to men. I sat down and wrote a list that I should have written years earlier to help me to be more cautious before jumping into my next relationship. I did notice that I was trying to change the men that came into my life and yet it was I who did all the changing, so I sat down and wrote the following list.

The perfect man for me will be stable, intelligent, educated, confident, secure in himself, competent in his business; he shall possess an inner strength, have a strong voice, must be sexy, financially secure, generous, someone who respects women and loves sports;

he must be eloquent, enjoy the finer things in life, have common sense, the ability to express his feelings, have manners, and he must love me very much.

As I finished writing this wish list, I realized that the qualities were lacking a physical description, so I added he must be tall, dark, and handsome. After I finished the list I reread it and realized there was still something missing; no mention of his being a good dad to my future children, maybe because the thought of a father had naturally been omitted from my mind. I promised myself to consult this list before my next relationship and placed it in my file titled, "Important Papers".

CHAPTER SEVEN

"Solid as a Rock"

Ashford and Simpson

It took time to recover from Marv and our divorce. I heard that he and Jennifer had gotten closer as a result of our failed marriage and I figured they deserved each other. Lori and I were living very peacefully with one another; even my cat and Lori's golden retriever Rockie were getting along as well. But I did question her choice of music.

"What are you listening to?" I asked.

"New Age music, it's spiritual. I meditate to it. I'll show you how if you want? Come on why don't you try it with me?"

"I can't, I'll never sit still long enough, but thanks anyway. Go ahead, enjoy and do some breathing for me." I responded, and we started cracking up.

Even though our thought process and personalities are very different, as young adults we agreed to disagree and accept each other for who we were as individuals, permitting us to remain close and have far fewer arguments.

My real estate career had skyrocketed. I had finally found my passion in the world of real estate and with that, I knew I would be successful. Finding out what you love to do is the hardest part, but once you find it, working hard becomes easier and is usually followed by triumph.

I was in the "zone" and one day one of my clients wanted a custom built home. After diligent research, I found the perfect builder for them. My clients were so happy and in the process of all the work and research I had done, the builder was impressed, too. One of the General Managers asked me to leave my company and exclusively represent them, selling their new subdivisions to potential new homeowners. Personally, this represented a great deal of prosperity to me on many levels; better benefits, more money faster and not nearly the legwork or driving that I had been doing. In addition, they would also pay me a draw against commission. It was perfect, but I was nevertheless torn because I loved my broker and they had done so much for me. My clientele was escalating and the referrals were flowing in left and right.

During negotiations, I asked my potential new boss if I could do both; stay with my current company and work for them too. She insisted that it would be impossible unless I was superwoman. After weighing both sides I decided it was an offer too good to refuse. My broker and co-workers gave me a beautiful going-away luncheon.

"We build it up and build it up and build it up."

Selling new construction ended up to be the success I was looking for. Over the next thirteen years, my career took off, earning me many gold and silver million dollar circle awards from the Builders Association. Because the subdivisions I represented continued to sell out on a timely basis, my bosses were ecstatic. During this time, I was able to save some serious money, which I designated to be a down payment on my very first home of my own.

My future was looking up. I had built a more secure life, and this was ultimately what I was seeking all along. My social life was almost non-existent, which was fine with me. My work became my life and even though I dated a bit here and there, I didn't realize that I was married to my career. I worked six days a week and loved every minute of it. If I was sure of anything, it was the fact that I would never, ever get married again.

In 1990, I began looking for my own home and decided on a condominium, which fit my lifestyle perfectly. I looked at several units, and then I found the one screaming my name. It was considered a greenbelt location, surrounded by hills and valleys with many trees. There was a garden area in front, a full basement and a one car attached garage. When I took Mom and Lori to see the condo, they loved it too. I was scheduled to close in about four weeks.

I had been living with my sister five wonderful years and it was the most stable life I had lived, since my late teens. One evening, before my move, I took a break from packing. Lori and I sat down on the sofa and had a glass of wine.

"I'm so scared, Lori; I never lived alone before. I've either had a husband, a roommate, or lived with you. And of course you have been my favorite," I said and we both giggled

"Oh, Dori, don't be so dramatic, you'll be fine. You are going to love it. The nice part is, you will know real freedom and you won't have anyone else to deal with," she said as Rockie came up and started licking my hand.

"Can I borrow her once in a while or maybe she could sleep over?" I asked

"No way, absolutely not! You'll have to get your own dog, and besides you have Samantha," she said adamantly.

"Fine, I will go out this weekend and buy my own dog, so there!" We both laughed and she agreed to go with me to find my very own Prince Charming.

"Ten Minutes Ago."

When I was talking with mom she mentioned a dog breed I may like, a bichon frisé, and suggested I take a look. The following Sunday, Lori and I went to the local pet store and there he was—a little white fluff ball no bigger than my hand.

"You looked up when I came through the door."

With his big black eyes staring at me and playfully jumping around, wagging his tail, I couldn't resist the urge to hold him. I spent ten minutes with him, and one look was all it took. I pulled out my credit card and took my little "Prince" home along with toys and treats galore.

I realized the next morning that I had to go to work and couldn't leave him alone, so I put him in his training crate and took him to work, keeping him under my desk for the first two years of his life. My clients loved him, which made my work life with Prince so much easier. My boss never knew I had him because my office was always on site of the property, away from management. If I learned that anyone from corporate was coming out to see me, I would leave Prince at home. I took him everywhere; he was always by my side.

It was a very exciting time for me, because I finally felt a sense of security; I was a homeowner and I had my dog who was here to stay. All I was missing was my handsome husband and my four children.

For the first month in my new home I felt as if I were living in a hotel. As I became more comfortable with my surroundings, I was able to move things around and put everything in its place. I furnished it with a black, white and taupe color scheme throughout. My Prince was beautiful, flawlessly white and matched the décor perfectly. I never gave him less than a million little kisses each day, and we were both so happy in our new life.

CHAPTER EIGHT

"That's What Friends Are For"

Dionne Warwick

A year or so had passed and as angry as I was at her, I really missed having Jennifer in my life. My last call to her had been out of disgust and pain. I simply wanted to hurt her with silence because the betrayal was unforgivable. Knowing Jen, she couldn't choose between Marv and me, which she didn't have to do anyway. So, befriending both of us caused her to lie to me and pacify Marvin at the same time. I was still angry, but my anger had softened.

The memory of our close friendship had outweighed the awful episode. She had tried to contact me in the past, but I stubbornly refused to acknowledge her. But now I was ready and wanted to get in touch with her.

In the past, every year her grandmother would send her a Chanukah card including a little *gelt* (a gift of money), so after her grandmother passed away, every December I would send her a card with a check and sign it with her grandmother's name. I did this for Jennifer because I loved the festivities, and Jennifer could always use the money. So, since it was the holiday season, I sent her a card signed, "Love, Grandma Laura" and waited, hoping that she would respond to me, and she did. She called me the day she received it, and we made plans to meet for dinner.

"I was so mixed up Dori; Marv kept pressuring me all the time. He had to know where you were and what you were doing. He was going nuts because you left him. I was the closest person to you and in a sick way that kept you a part of him. And now someone was finally paying attention to me, even though it was for all the wrong reasons. I was worn out from his questions, and I made a huge mistake for divulging your whereabouts. I'm so very sorry."

After we talked back and forth expressing my anger and her apologies, we ended up crying and hugging until all was forgiven. It would still be another year for me to really let go of the memories of an angry past filled with her betrayal.

Jennifer and Marv had become very close friends, which was no surprise to me and actually made a lot of sense. They were very much alike in many ways and had so much in common, especially me.

"Knowin' you can always count on me, for sure."

My friendship with Jennifer took some time to rebuild. It required patience on both our parts and eventually we were back as if nothing had ever happened between us. I never blamed her for my breakup with Marv; our marriage was headed for the rocks. She too struggled because she was a friend to both of us and it hurt her to see us divorced.

At this point, Mom had met a man in California while on vacation and fell in love; she and Harry ended up relocating to Arizona. They had a beautiful private wedding conducted by the one and only Rabbi Stein.

Lori and I were not able to attend the wedding so we offered to throw them a party here in Detroit with all our friends and family to honor their marriage. All they had to do was show up. When they arrived we had a wonderful celebration. It was nice to see her again and to finally see her happy. I had an opportunity to meet Harry and get to know him better, since they stayed with me. They both enjoyed their time in Detroit before flying back home.

I got the chance to visit them in Arizona at least once a year, and always had a wonderful time. I felt as if I had real parents because their focus was on me. I felt safe, secure, and like the most important little girl in the world. This was something I had never known before and I loved every minute. Sometimes during my visit, Mom encouraged me and even dragged me out to the singles clubs, but I wasn't interested. All I wanted was to spend time with her and Harry. He was a kind, warm and gentle man. He was so good to all of us and I loved him very much. Often he would send Lori and me gifts with handwritten notes.

Dear Dori,

I hope you like the beige blazer; it will look so good on you. Your mother and I are doing fine and the weather here in Phoenix is beautiful. I'm trying to teach her how to play golf and maybe I can teach you too? We enjoyed your last visit and we can't wait until your next one. Missing you always, Love Harry

1993 became my best financial year ever. Having been active in the real estate business for over six years, I still wanted more. I went back to school, became a broker and opened my own brokerage firm. My income continued to grow to six figures and I was in demand and felt so proud. I found confidence and comfort with who I was becoming. Yet, the gnawing feeling of something missing left me unsettled. It seemed all the men I had chosen to be with were losers. It had occurred to me that this could very well be my own fault.

Mom had come in for a visit from Phoenix. Harry couldn't make it because he was in a golf tournament. She had heard Max Stein had become a concert pianist and he was performing at a local outdoor theatre.

"Dori, would you like to go see him Friday night? I heard he was fabulous, and you haven't seen him since you were fifteen years old," she asked.

"Mom, remember when he took me out for dinner and I ate those vile grape leaves? The only good thing was he was the rabbi's son," I said.

"Yes, but that was a long time ago. Come on Dori, let's go see him, it will be fun and something different," Mom persisted.

After a little coaxing, she convinced me to go and hear him play. Oh my G-d, I was going to pay good money to listen to Max Stein, the man who made me eat grape leaves so many years ago during the time I worked at Temple Hadera.

Max had graduated from Juilliard and then went on to become a concert pianist. He was well traveled and famous. He could play any song from classical to soul without a sheet of music in front of him. It was a beautiful night weather-wise for Michigan, perfect for an outdoor concert.

As we were listening to Max play his concertos in awe, my (not usually pushy) mom leaned over and said,

"Dori, after the show, why don't you go up to the stage and simply say hello?"

"I'm not interested. Was this your ulterior motive?" I asked angrily.

"I know you're not interested, but you should do it anyway," she insisted, while ignoring my question.

The concert was fabulous. After the show and with a little more coaxing from Mom, I went up to the stage to see him. I felt so embarrassed, and I certainly didn't look my best. Max was standing at the far right of the stage shaking people's hands. As I stood in his direct eyesight, he recognized me and smiled. We met halfway, and he gave me a big hug. He thanked me for coming to his concert and then quietly asked me for my number, which I gave him and he promised to call. He kissed me on the cheek and went back to the well wishers to shake their hands.

I returned to my seat where mom was waiting in silent expectation. She nodded calmly and then not able to hold back, she hugged me, while beaming with pride that her game plan had worked.

Max called the next day, Saturday. He assumed I was busy and I just let him think that. We made plans for dinner on Monday night. I was excited about our reunion. Things were different now so the age difference didn't seem as drastic. He was a man and a famous one at that. He was also the son of the most admired rabbi in our community who was also very special to me.

Max came to pick me up with a bouquet of flowers in his hand. We had a wonderful dinner and our conversation seemed to go on forever. Upon returning home, he asked me out for the following Saturday and I accepted. After that, we began dating regularly and I was having the time of my life. I hadn't dated anyone seriously in about two years— actually since my divorce from Marv. Up until now I just wasn't interested.

One evening, after Max had moved back into town, we were at his parent's house where he was staying temporarily. We were sipping wine and cuddling on the couch when the rabbi came downstairs and gave me a hug.

"I can't wait until you are my daughter-in-law," he would whisper to me.

I loved the rabbi and would love more than anything to be a part of this family. However, I still had my doubts about getting into another relationship and didn't trust Max or anyone else.

We dated for about six months and one night, when I was all dressed up waiting for him, he called to tell me he was running late. Two hours later, I was still waiting and my makeup had started to wilt. He called again and claimed to have car trouble and asked me to pick him up.

I was out the door in less than a minute. It never occurred to me that I was once again in the rescuing mode. When I saw him in person, I noticed he was acting strange and distant. He seemed preoccupied, anxious, and his forehead was damp with sweat.

"What is wrong with you?" I asked sincerely. "I'm sure I can help you, just tell me what it is."

"Dori, I will tell you everything at dinner, but you have to drive," he said.

"OK, no problem." I said.

We left the house and I asked him where he wanted to go for dinner. The first few minutes in the car were silent, until he blurted out his confession.

"I met someone else and I can't see you anymore."

"What? What did you say? How could you? Why? How? When did this happen?" Blubbering like an idiot, I quickly took my eyes off the road to look at him. As my eyes filled with tears blurring my vision, I pulled off the road into a hotel parking lot. We walked into the hotel restaurant; he tried to explain himself, while apologizing left and right.

"I'm so sorry Dori, but this woman I met is much older than you and she doesn't want to have any children." He rambled on, though we had never talked about marriage or children for that matter.

"She is also going to manage my career and take it to a higher level," he continued.

I began to feel nauseous and sweaty. I definitely didn't want to hear about his new girlfriend. However, what I gathered from all of this was he found another mother to take care of him. This was why he moved back home. We never ate dinner, and I drove him back home in silence, while I brooded over the pain and infidelity. I waited until he got out of the car and heard the final sound of him closing the door. I drove off, knowing I would never hear from him again.

My heart was heavy and the only sounds I heard now were my own sighs of pain. I couldn't believe he had the nerve to leave me. No one had ever left me except my dad. I also knew that I would get over him, and, in due time, I would clean myself up and dust myself off once again.

I talked with mom the next morning and she was shocked and upset, too.

"Mom, when is it going to happen?" I asked her, but this time I knew the answer.

In the simple words of a Doris Day song, "Que Sera, Sera, the future's not ours to see. Que Sera, Sera."

"Dori, you are only thirty nine years old," she said. I began working out at a local health club to get rid of my anxiety. I heard that Max did marry the other, older woman within a year. I vowed in my bruised heart that I was done with men forever.

About a year later, I went to Temple Hadera for Shabbat services on a Friday night to hear Rabbi Stein deliver his sermon. After the service, I went up to him to say hello. He gave me the tightest and warmest hug ever.

"I'm so sorry, Dori dear; I don't know what got into my son. Please remember one thing for the rest of your life; without respect or trust you have no love." He kissed me on the cheek and gave me his blessings. I wished him the same. A few months later, I received a letter from the rabbi that read,

"One of these days, a man worthy enough will find you and appreciate all the wonderful qualities you possess. Kindest regards and much love, Rabbi Stein"

I've cherished this letter ever since, and I hope one day I will be able to say "Thank you" because a worthy man did find me. Despite my vow of not dating men anymore, I did date again. In fact, I dated two guys for a very short time. The first guy gave me an ultimatum after a couple of months. "You have a choice to make. It's either me or the dog, who's it going to be?"

That was an easy decision. I left telling him to have a nice life. The second guy told me he was allergic to condoms.

"Oh really, is that so? Well I'm allergic to you. Have a nice life," I replied. There are so many jerks out there, and I seemed to meet all of them.

CHAPTER NINE

Help

The Beatles

It was a typical January in Michigan; cold, gloomy, and icy. Yet it was a significant year, in that I was turning forty. I had just spoken with Mom, and we toyed with the idea of my moving to Phoenix to be closer to her and Harry. It was a good idea since winters were a lot warmer in Phoenix, and I really had nothing holding me in Detroit.

So, I went ahead and updated my résumé and designed a cover letter just to get some feelers out there to see what the job market was like. I didn't want to up and move if there were no job prospects, so I mailed out a bunch of résumés. The feedback was tremendous. Because of the great response, I booked my flight and set up a string of interviews. Thinking in advance, I decided I would rent out my condo in lieu of selling it, just to be on the safe side. I found a management company that could manage the rental and locate potential new tenants if I were to follow through on the move.

About ten days later, I landed in sunny Phoenix, Arizona where the picturesque mountains take your breath away. Harry drove me to all of my interviews and I managed to narrow it down to one company. I went in for a second interview; I was excited about it, as if I were a teenager getting her first car.

I went through the second interview with flying colors and did well on any and every test they threw at me. They were an incredibly thorough company and offered me a job selling new homes in this huge retirement community, and my income would be over the top. Everything was perfect about the job, except for one thing; I didn't love Phoenix. For the first time in my life I began to question my motives for making a change. The only reason I was out there was because I was lonely, and I could live near Mommy and Daddy. *But what if Mommy and Daddy moved away?* It would just be me, the weird-looking cacti, and the mountains. So I declined the job, knowing that I could visit Mom and Harry as often as I wanted.

On the flight back to Detroit I felt at peace with my decision. When the plane landed it felt good to be home again. Jennifer was thrilled that I didn't take the job, and she began preparing for my birthday.

"What do you want to do for the big birthday?" she asked.

"Surprise me," I told her and smiled.

Turning forty felt a lot better than I had expected. I remember how depressed I was when I turned thirty. I guess it all depends on where you are in your life.

Jennifer and Marv were now living together and she was content, which in turn made me happy. I loved Jennifer, but I didn't want him to be a part of my life whatsoever. He was in my past where he belonged. I guess it was due to the earlier problems that I never totally got the suspicion out of my mind that she still shared my every move with him.

Prince and I did some volunteer work visiting nursing homes and orphanages. It was a wonderful program and he loved the attention. Much like his owner, he was very social. He brightened the day of everyone he met and covered them in wet sloppy kisses. It was a very rewarding experience for the both of us.

Jennifer had made special plans for my birthday. We were going to dine at my favorite Greek restaurant, Big Daddy's, with a few close friends along with Lori and my cousin Kathy. I had a brand new outlook on life. I was comfortable mentally, spiritually and physically. I promised myself never to be a rescuer again. This birthday represented more then turning a year older; it was a celebration of freedom and to a degree, healing.

We were having a wonderful time, and I received some great gifts as well as enjoying the juicy lamb chops. Jennifer waved to a friend of hers seated at the opposite end of the restaurant. His name was Jerry and he came to our table and joined us for a drink. I instantly felt an attraction to this man.

Soon after my birthday, Jerry and I began dating. He had a dynamite personality; he was very good looking, with a fantastic body. We'd go driving in his little red sports car and we'd have a lot of fun. He was an artist and also sold commercial real estate, so we had more than just a physical attraction in common.

We went out for a few weeks and then suddenly he stopped calling me. I wasn't about to call him; obviously he wasn't interested. Mom raised me never to chase boys, let them do the chasing.

Nevertheless, I was frustrated and upset over the situation. But I vowed I wasn't going to fall apart over him or any man ever again. I had acquired a new "I don't care attitude;" after all, I was never getting married again. After a couple of weeks Jerry would call and we would start over where we left off. This pattern of Jerry's inconsistency went on for six months. I pretended it didn't hurt me, and I wouldn't let his behavior drive me crazy. Until, finally I asked him, "Why are you so on and off with me?"

"I really care about you Dori. However, I can't start a new chapter in my life until I close the old one," Jerry said, coming clean.

"What chapter are you talking about?" I asked, confused by his words.

"I'm still married. My estranged wife and I are leading separate lives, and I can't pretend to be a single man anymore. I'm very sorry," he said sheepishly, while looking down with shame.

How could I have been so blind? Oh my G-d, I'm definitely allergic to men!

I thought I had it all together, but I couldn't have been more wrong. However, this time was different; I refused to clean myself up and dust myself off. I was finally angry enough, and I swore in my heart this would never happen to me again.

I felt men and marriage were not in the cards for me, and I didn't need a man to be happy. But I could do something about desperately wanting to have a baby, and I was certainly running out of time. So I directed my energies to being a single parent and I planned to begin investigating sperm banks instead of spending time at the mall. I had my guest room available, which I could convert into a nursery, and I had enough money to make it work. I explained the entire Jerry fiasco to Mom, and she suggested I seek some professional counseling. I sighed, because I knew she was right but didn't want to admit it. Then after speaking with Lori, she suggested the same thing. Surely the two supportive, loving women in my life couldn't be wrong.

"Now I find I've changed my
mind and opened up the doors."

So, after a few days of bemoaning my two failed marriages and more than enough bad boyfriends, I picked up my ruby red doctor referral book and laughed because I was still searching for the right man.

It was the end of a beautiful day in June of 1995 when I made an appointment with Dr. Kaplan. It felt as if the appointment day had snuck up on me, and there I stood at the door of his office. I was extremely apprehensive about the whole thing.

The place was drab and plain-looking with a couple of brown chairs and a small wood table to match. A single white button was mounted on the wall. I reached to push it and then I hesitated, contemplating running out of there. But then with a big sigh I pushed the button, expecting to hear a doorbell, but there was silence. Moments later, the door opened and Dr. Kaplan smiled, introduced himself and invited me in. He was a tall, older, dignified Jewish man. I gathered my composure and followed him into his office. I felt as if I were there to interview him and see if he was the right man for the job. I had my doubts since my ability to judge the characteristics of a person had always been clouded.

"How may I help you?" he asked in a soft, gentle voice. He sat back in his huge black leather chair; I sat across from him next to a big box of tissues. His office was clearly set up to define the patient/doctor relationship.

"Well, first of all, the only reason I'm here is because my mother and sister think I need help. I'm also looking for a role model and mentor because I have no clue as to what makes men tick. And just so you know, I'm never getting married again," I said honestly.

Then I went on about my career, home life, and Prince. *I can't believe I'm saying all this to a total stranger.*

"I hope that covers it, and I believe you're the one to help me," I stated.

Dr. Kaplan listened intently, his eyes staring right to the heart of me, while patiently waiting until I was finished. Then he leaned forward and asked, "Why have you chosen me?"

"Because I have never had a male role model; you are a man, medium age, and Jewish. And I think you could help me figure out what I'm doing wrong in the men department."

"You don't always have to have immediate solutions to your problems. You have to evaluate your situations first, even when it comes to choosing a man or a doctor. By taking this approach you will have an educated decision, without any regrets. And as far as you not needing or wanting a man in your life, you shouldn't miss out on having the experience and the intensity of the greatest feeling in the world, which is being in love and being loved in return," he said.

Wow, this man has my full attention. Okay he's evaluated. After our first session, I knew he was the right therapist for me.

Our next session went pretty well and my beliefs were reaffirmed; he was the one man I would learn from and besides, I was open to it and the timing felt right. I wasn't used to the patient/doctor relationship and I tried to create a more casual friendly atmosphere.

"How are you?" I asked him before we began.

"These sessions are about you, not me," he responded in his professional voice. He set the boundary lines early on and demanded respect. He showed it to me loud and clear. This was hard because I wanted to know more about him, yet he preferred to keep a safe distance emotionally and personally from me, which after a period of time, I learned to understand and accept.

Our sessions really had no order, but usually began with recent events and then I would bounce back and forth from the past to the present. I expected him to want to know everything all the way back to my birth, like the teachings of Dr. Sigmund Freud. We had been talking about my teen years when the issue of using drugs came up.

"I could have easily been on hard drugs growing up," I said.

"You didn't have the luxury to be irresponsible because there was no one to pick up the pieces if you did. If you had thrown in the towel, you wouldn't have the life you have today."

"But what about the men I have chosen in my life? What's wrong with me?" I asked.

"My careers have always been successful and I have done very well, yet my relationships, especially husbands have been disastrous." I added. *Where's that*

Kleenex box? "It's not the men, Dori. It's you. You chose them based on what you witnessed as a child. This was a learned behavior starting at birth, directly from your biological father. He ended up being strictly the sperm donor and it ended there," he said with compassion.

I listened to him intently as he went on to describe my dad as if he knew him personally.

"Your dad was weak, needy, and wanted to be saved and cared for by anyone who was within reach. There was no way he could have taken care of your mom, Lori, or you."

Over the next few months, we worked on the intricate details of my past and how I handled them. I was really opening up, and I was encouraged to know that there was hope. He had helped me put the people in my life and my decisions into a brand new perspective. I wasn't supposed to rescue others or please them and I learned that the decisions that others make, and the consequences that follow, are not my responsibility, but theirs.

Dr. Kaplan gave me a great education about myself and about life in general. Though he admitted he couldn't take away the problems, he could teach me how to handle them and make better decisions in the future. With his help I was going to live a healthier life and move forward and evaluate people and situations before making a decision in sixty seconds. I no longer had to accept something just because it was offered. I had the power to choose, and that empowered me in a mighty way.

Dr. Kaplan knew when to pursue answers and when to back off. He was a sensitive, caring man who really was looking out for my best interest. He didn't dwell on my past, but taught me a way to cope with the situations of the present. This freed me from reliving my past and dwelling on it. I was living in the now for the first time in my life with a clear understanding of what went on a long time ago. My past will never interfere with my life again, I refuse to let it. I told Dr. Kaplan that working with him was like winning the million dollar lottery of life. I ended up cherishing our many sessions and finally felt liberated. Dr. Kaplan announced,

"Well Dori, this it, I know you can go live your life wisely and you don't need me anymore."

"What? I'm ready to graduate!" We both laughed.

I looked at him blankly and felt a sense of disappointment, like watching a tire going flat in slow motion.

Dr. Kaplan had become a mentor to me, the only one I ever had. The next session would be our last, and I decided to bring my camera to take his picture, assuming he wouldn't mind.

"You don't need a photograph of me. You will remember me in your mind's eye," he assured me and went on to encourage me not to give up on the idea of marriage.

"It is very easy to find the wrong man; the hard part is finding the right one. Happiness will follow you, Dori, when the right man comes along. Don't ever settle. You deserve the best there is," he said as we parted company. He told me to call him if I ever needed him. I left his office sad, but not empty. With tears rolling down my face, I realized I never got to know him personally, and this stranger will forever remain in my mind's eye.

I looked back to when my therapy began, remembering how weak I felt, so vulnerable and so very foolish. But afterwards I held my head up high, feeling strong and confident that I was finished screwing up.

All I wanted to do now was move forward and begin living again with a fresh, new, healthier start and to continue 'Singing the Song of Life'. I was excited to know what would happen next and how I would respond to it.

CHAPTER TEN

"Papa Was a Rolling Stone"

The Temptations

In early fall of 1995, I felt good about who I was becoming, along with my very successful career. I was never more vibrant, more confidant and, most importantly, thanks to Dr. Kaplan, more emotionally free. I no longer had to wear a pretend happy face. My smile was coming from within, not because of what others wanted to see.

Once in a while I would think of Dr. Kaplan sitting in his high backed, leather chair and the image always brought a tender smile to my face. Everything and everyone in my life was stable and strong. Mom and Lori were doing well, and Prince was my ever-faithful companion. Jennifer and Marv were still together and very happy.

"Where ever he laid his hat was his home."

One day my cousin Kathy called me and mentioned that my dad was very ill and was moving back to Detroit to live with my Aunt Darlene.

My dad had *myasthenia gravis*, a disease that caused a deterioration of the muscles which can be controlled with medication. She told me he was driving his old pickup from Florida and would arrive in a few days.

After our conversation I had this unexplainable need to see him. Maybe it was all the things that I learned from Dr. Kaplan, or maybe I wanted to see how I would respond now that I had found healing from the past. I waited a few days until he got settled in and called to set up a time to visit with him. I invited Lori, but she had no desire to see him, so I went alone.

"Folks say Papa never was much on thinking."

I shouldn't have been shocked by his appearance, but I was. It had been a few decades, but I never expected to see him so worn out and haggard. He was a frail, unkempt old man and our visit consisted of meaningless small talk. I felt uncomfortable talking to my dad because he felt like a stranger.

Daddy, why did you leave us, didn't you care? Why weren't you there to hold me, and let me sit on your lap so I could tell you my problems, while kissing my forehead and telling me everything will be alright? Why weren't you there to read me a story and tuck me in at night? Why would you deprive me of being whole? Why did you divorce me, what did I do wrong? I didn't finish college Dad, too many outstanding government loans. Why didn't you let me love you? Why didn't you love me? The severe pain was becoming so unbearable from my increasingly powerful thoughts that I was afraid my internal terror was going to explode, and I had to do something quick. I abruptly said; "I have to go Dad." I couldn't spend another moment with him. When I left, I vowed not to see him alone ever again.

A few days later, he called and invited Lori and me out for coffee and we went. I felt strong enough to handle it and was kind of happy about the possibility of his being a part of my life again. I had to be cautious and wanted to protect my emotions and keep them intact. I accepted who he was and maybe, just maybe, I could fill the one piece of my pie that had been missing all my life, a father. Even if that piece was only half-baked.

"So, do you want to know what I have been doing for the last forty years?" I asked sarcastically. We all laughed, yet we knew it wasn't funny. Lori sat and listened, barely saying a word. The three of us ended up meeting for coffee once a week. This lasted five short weeks. He wanted to be the big shot and always treated.

"Girls, I have a favor to ask you," he said as we were enjoying our coffee.

Inside I was getting ready for the bomb to hit. I knew it was coming.

"Go ahead, Dad. Ask."

"I need to borrow thirty-seven dollars from each of you girls," he said with a weak smile.

As I pulled out my checkbook, the hope I had was gone, but I also knew how strong I had become and wrote a check out for the full $74.00. As I handed the check to him, Lori and I both exchanged glances. We knew that our father-daughter coffee meetings were over and this was simply a good deed—never to see the money again. I had passed my first test and was emotionally still in one piece.

CHAPTER ELEVEN

"The Sound of Silence"

Simon and Garfunkel

One early fall evening my friend Marilee and I went to our favorite restaurant. We couldn't wait to sit down to eat because we had a lot of things to catch up on. Marilee was happily married to a really nice guy, and she wanted the same happiness for me.

"My life is fine the way it is. I've never been happier," I told her in all honesty.

Physically, I felt like a beautiful woman. I was thin, had long blonde hair and my nails were the perfect length. And though I longed to wear a string bikini, my body hasn't caught up yet. It was an important goal to me and finally it was in reach.

I was wearing my tight, black stretch jeans, which made me feel sexy and attractive. Life really did begin at forty. The risks that I took in my twenties and the caution that I demonstrated in my thirties were replaced by the confidence I had entering my forties. I was so excited to see what the next few decades would bring.

As Marilee and I continued our girl talk, I couldn't help but glance at a gorgeous man standing by the bar and talking with the owner. I watched as he gently inhaled his cigarette and couldn't believe how my thoughts began to race ahead of me. Marilee looked at me and the man who stole my attention from her.

"And the vision that was planted
in my brain still remains."

"He *is* gorgeous!" she said with enthusiasm.
I nodded, lighting up a cigarette. When I looked back at him, we made eye contact, and then I felt butterflies in my stomach. I was blushing and I knew my eyes lit up at the thought of his looking at me. The waitress broke the trance as she came and took our orders.

Throughout our meal, I kept an eye on him as he did me. Since we had a lot of food left over, the waitress gave us carryout boxes. As we collected and packed up the food, I saw some people whom I knew and went up to talk with them. The room was so crowded that people had to squeeze to get by, and that's exactly what this handsome man did to get by me. As we exchanged smiles, I was feeling a little warmer than I had been all evening.

When I returned to the table, Marilee had a mile wide smile on her face.

"Let's take our carryout boxes to the car, then come back and sit at the bar for some coffee," she suggested. Minutes later we were sitting at the bar.

Marilee took charge and guided me to the opposite end of the bar from where this handsome man was standing. He was about 6' tall, with curly, dark, wavy hair and a mustache. He was wearing jeans and a tan sports jacket with brand new white walking shoes.

"Now what do we do, my friend the matchmaker?" I asked her as we waited for our cappuccinos, casting glances at him as he looked at me from the corner of his eye.

"Well, I could simply tell him you want to meet him," she said coyly.

"Absolutely not! I got it; I'll do the ladies' room trick. You know, casually walking by him and see what happens."

Feeling clever I stood up, straightened my top and then nonchalantly walked by him. As we made eye contact, I stopped dead in my tracks and looked directly at him.

"You look familiar!" I lied.

I wanted to break the sound of silence that stood between us like a gigantic wall made out of bricks of fear and layers of mortar filled with insecurities.

"Hi, I'm Ari Winger, and you are?" he said extending his hand.

As I shook his strong but soft hand, I could feel he had some muscle under his shirt.

"I'm Dori Silverstein, nice to meet you." I moved towards the bar and began talking. Quickly, we found out we had a great deal in common. I had my own real estate brokerage firm, and he was in commercial real estate.

"Maybe that's why you look familiar," I said and we both laughed.

"How many people in your real estate group, Dori?"

"One," I answered bashfully.

"How many in your group, Ari?"

"Just one," he answered, as we both cracked up again. After a few minutes I realized I had forgotten Marilee who was watching us and nodding her head in approval at the other end of the bar. I asked Ari if he wanted to join me and Marilee for coffee. He agreed and the three of us sat at the bar and within a few minutes, as if on cue, Marilee said she had to leave. I knew exactly what she was doing, and I felt very nervous about her leaving so abruptly.

"Call me tomorrow," she said on her way out. We watched her leave and after a few moments of awkward silence, we began talking and continued for about an hour. I checked my watch and said, "It's time for me to go; I have to get up for work in the morning. You know, the real estate business keeps us busy seven days a week."

"Can I get your number?" Ari asked gently.

"Sure," I said with a smile and wrote my number on the back of my business card, handed it to him, and we shook hands. *What soft hands he has.* I left with a huge smile on my face and a glimmer of hope in my heart.

On Saturday, when I got home from work I kicked off my shoes and listened to my messages while I let Prince outside. I stared at the answering machine when I heard his voice.

"Hi Dori, this is Ari Winger. We met last night. I wanted to know if you'd like to have dinner with me Tuesday evening. I'll call you tomorrow for your answer or you can give me a call back at 810.123.4567."

It was the only message I had all day and I would have called him back, except of course it was Saturday night and heaven forbid I should be home.

So I waited and called him on Sunday and accepted his dinner invitation.

My heart jumped when the doorbell rang. It was Ari, right on time with a bouquet of flowers. I invited him in, thinking we were going to leave right away, but he sat on the sofa; he looked tired. So I offered him a drink, and we both sat and had cocktails before leaving for dinner.

Ari had made reservations at a wonderful jazz club where we were seated in a cozy leather booth and ordered dinner while enjoying the music that seemed to echo from the walls. I hadn't noticed immediately but we had been holding hands the entire time. Our first date ended with a long, hot, tingly kiss goodnight at my door.

"I'll call you," he said and I smiled. *That's what they all say.*

My anticipation was renewed when he called the next day for a date on Saturday. I so wanted to see him again. Saturday night couldn't have come fast enough. After a time of relaxing at my place, we went to dinner at a café. I noticed a lot of people knew Ari. He had a long history in the city; this was a good sign to me. Yet I couldn't help sensing a certain sadness that overshadowed his otherwise smiling face.

"The long and winding road."

His mother and father had miraculously managed to escape Hitler during the Holocaust and relocate to Israel. His dad became a sergeant major and fought on the front lines. When he discovered that his two brothers were still alive and living in the United States, he immediately traveled to America in search of them, leaving behind his wife and two children.

While his father was away, Ari had become the man of the house at eight years old. For the next two years he went out and worked to help support his mom and younger sister, Lydia. He managed to find a job picking peanuts, but since he was always hungry he ate most of his profits. Because of his childhood, or lack of one, he had a deep appreciation for life. He did what was necessary to help his family survive. Two years later, his father sent for them. His family was poor, and Ari couldn't speak a word of English.

Ari was ten years old when he came to America, and his first six months were the toughest. Since he didn't speak any English, he was somewhat of an outcast and often felt the brunt of cruel jokes from the other kids. He would get beat up just because he was different. Once his father heard about it, he showed Ari how to fight back. After he fought back, the kids soon learned to leave him alone.

By the time he was thirteen, three years later, he had fully adapted to the American lifestyle. He was fluent in English and knew he wanted to be a doctor. As he grew older, he learned, enjoyed, and had a knack for winning money at playing pool. His talent for the game became his part-time job. He was considered a pool shark and was able to earn some serious money, which he put away for college and medical school. He also worked part time in delicatessens and fruit markets to earn extra money. After graduating from high school, he spent a year in college, but his desire for financial freedom became a priority, and he said good-bye to his dream of being a doctor.

At the age of nineteen, he took in a partner and opened his first deli. After a few years of very hard work, he gained an unbelievable amount of knowledge. He also went through a few more partners and a few different delis, where he gained priceless experience. At twenty-three years old, he opened a two hundred-seat, multi million-dollar delicatessen. He named it "Corned Beef and Rye". It was a huge success and became a major part of the social scene in Southfield, Michigan. I didn't spend much time eating there, but my mom and sister did.

Ari was a really good guy. He was fondly thought of and well-liked throughout the community. As we continued to talk and get to know each other, we found our lives had been parallel to one another. Socially, we went to identical places and we knew a lot of the same people. However, for some reason, our paths had never crossed. I also noticed, along with the things we had in common and the obvious physical attraction, there was something else going on. My feelings were different, very foreign to me. He seemed somewhat reserved, but very intense and a deep thinker. So when he spoke, I listened. In the meantime, I was evaluating him by taking it slow and keeping my distance physically, but the chemistry between us was driving me crazy. He showed me a great deal of respect while our dates ended the same way, with a luscious kiss at my door and inviting him in, only this time he declined and said, "I'll call you tomorrow."

I watched him leave, but couldn't get him off of my mind. We had been dating about two weeks when he took me to his friend's house to introduce me. This made me feel so important as I watched him beam with pride. His gentle behavior was very refreshing.

After that he took me to his ex-wife's place of employment to meet her, which made me want to put up a wall of protection. *Why does he still need her approval?* This seemed weird but harmless, and she was very pleasant. In the past I always ignored the clues and I'm learning to evaluate, I will speak to Ari about this later.

Dr. Kaplan gave me many tools to deal with life, and I was not about to float through another relationship foolishly wearing those ridiculous rose-colored glasses. I had slowed down to assess Ari, and I had decided in my heart that, if there proved to be a problem, it is not mine to fix. *Did I just say that?* I also had a keener judgment of people which was a tremendous help in my relationships, new and old. Ari explained he had been divorced twice and his second wife had sought companionship elsewhere. When he learned of it, his world came crashing down. He had thought that working hard and providing financial security for his family would be enough. Because of the shock of his eight-year-old marriage ending in such a way, he promised himself to never marry again.

After his divorce was final, he buried himself in his business because it offered him an escape from all he was going through. However, his empire began to tumble. He felt trapped, as if his business had become a prison and then sold the entire enterprise. About six months after the sale, the buyers defaulted and fled the country, nowhere to be found. This caused him great financial hardship, but the love of his children kept him going.

While my personal life was looking better, my work life was taking a turn for the worse. The builder for whom I was selling homes was becoming irrational and neurotic, making erratic decisions. I became increasingly uncomfortable and very unhappy representing him. Even my clients were having a difficult time with him. To top it off, he began arguing with me about one particular deal, and he refused to pay me my commission. The turning point came when he came into the office, looked at the renderings of the floor plans that hung beautifully on the wall, and began yelling at them.

"Why are you crooked? What's wrong with you?" he yelled.

I watched frozen in my tracks and said nothing, for fear of retaliation. I realized this was more than just a bad day. My life could be at risk and I decided to leave after we closed that night. I called Ari to explain my boss's erratic behavior and said, "I can't go out tonight, I'm too upset."

"That's fine, honey. Take it easy and everything will be all right," he said, while reassuring me.
When I hung up the phone, I thought of how kind and reassuring he had been.

I arrived home that night with my office in a cardboard box. As I drove up to the garage, there was a brightly colored gift bag leaning against my garage door. I quickly stopped my car and got out to grab the bag. I pulled out a card and read it.

"I'm sorry you had a terrible day, I hope this makes it better." It was signed, "Ari."

I pulled a small jewelry box from the bag and couldn't open it fast enough. It was a beautiful necklace and matching earrings. My mouth fell open in shock. It was such a thoughtful display of affection. He was the first man to show me a genuine selfless gesture and this felt incredible.

A few of my neighbors were outside and I ran to show them, forgetting about my idling car. I told them about my day and then showed them the gift from Ari. All of them agreed that 'he was a keeper'.

"The world will pardon my mush
Cause I've got a crush, my baby, on you."

After calming down a bit I pulled into the garage and unloaded my box of office supplies. Immediately, I called him to let him know how much I appreciated his thoughtfulness.

Ari and I began seeing each other more often, at least two to three times a week. Having cocktails at my house before going out for the evening had become the norm for us. The more time we spent together, the more I liked him, and the feeling appeared mutual. He invited me to join him and his family to go to the synagogue for services during the Jewish holidays, which touched my heart deeply.

"A touch of the past."

Ari had four children; two adult children from his first marriage, and two younger ones from his second marriage. He had an apartment with three bedrooms, so both of the younger children had their own room when they stayed with him. I admired how much he loved his kids and wanted to be a major part of their lives. During their weekly visits, he would often call me and his daughter would get on the phone.

"When are we going to meet you, Dori?" she would ask, her sweet voice ringing with such innocence.

"Soon honey," I would assure her.

I was in no rush. We were not even close to getting serious, and I didn't want the kids to get hurt any more than they had been. I had no idea where this relationship was going or even if it would work out. I knew somewhat of the trauma they had been through during their parents' divorce and did not want to add to it in anyway.

144

After his business went under, Ari, being the responsible dad that he was, took a job working as a counter man at a deli owned by a dear friend. He asked me to stop in and see him, but I only went once. I hated to see him working so hard for someone else when he had tasted so much success on his own.

He was also consulting and selling commercial real estate on the side. It was then I realized all the pressures he felt which caused the sadness that overshadowed his face. Since he was a workaholic, he vested a great deal of self-worth in his everyday life, no matter what role he played.

Ari had learned at an early age that you often have to start over more than once. He believed that starting at square one, hard work and loving what you do would virtually guarantee success. He had a great reputation. He was well liked and respected by many people. He also had their positive support, which enabled him to be such an encouragement to me. Finally, for the first time, I was enjoying a man for all the right reasons. I liked him for who he was and nothing else mattered.

The more we dated, the more intense our physical attraction grew for each other. He would bring me home from our night out and I would say the usual, "I have to go to sleep."

This frustrated him to no end. However, I continued playing hard-to-get and kept the intense heat stirring up between us. I was crazy about him, but I knew a lot of women had come and gone in his life, and I wanted to be different. I liked him too much to make it so easy. Besides, playing hard-to-get can be much more exciting. One night we went to our favorite casual diner and almost immediately after walking in, he grabbed my hand and pulled me out the door.

"What's wrong?" I asked totally puzzled by his behavior.

"We have to go somewhere else, I'll explain later," he said as we got into the car.

My heart began to race. He explained that his former girlfriend was at the bar. She had broken up with him three weeks before we met, but she had been calling him constantly and leaving him messages.

"She knows that I met someone new, and have moved on with my life. But now her niece, who used to work for me, is trying to get us back together."

I clearly understood why he was so upset and even embarrassed by having to explain the manipulation of his former girlfriend. But we managed to have a delightful dinner in spite of it.

After a few months, Ari gave me a dose of my own "playing hard-to-get" medicine. After another great evening he brought me home as per usual. He pulled up in front of my condo and instead of shutting off the engine like he always did he left it running, got out and opened my door to let me out. I started to panic; normally he would come in for a nightcap, then I would play my teasing game and he would leave.

"Aren't you coming in?" I asked as I got out of the car.

"No. The only way I will come in is if I can borrow your alarm clock," he said, while expressing a look that said "I gotcha.'"

I stood looking at him and smiled. *Yep, he was giving me a taste of my own medicine.* I stared at him for a moment in silence.

"Okay, fine, you can borrow my alarm clock," I told him with a nervous smile on my face.

Ari and I had the most amazingly wild and wonderful time getting to know each other more intimately.

146

Early the next morning, I looked over at this gorgeous man and I couldn't believe that we had finally made love and now he was sleeping peacefully next to me. It had been a long time since I had made love with a man and I was a little nervous, to say the least. Ari later admitted in the morning that he too, had been nervous.

Our relationship drastically changed and had gone to a new level. We spoke on the phone every day and tried to see each other whenever and wherever possible. Often, we would talk at night. I would lie in bed with the phone close to my ear and listen to his smooth sexy voice. Clutching my pillow, I would pretend he was next to me.

"My kids really want to meet you, Dori, what do you think?"

I was hesitant at first, thinking it was still too early, but then finally agreed.

A couple days later I walked into the Coney Island restaurant where Ari had set up our meeting. I immediately saw him with his beautiful thirteen-year-old daughter, Renee and his handsome eight-year-old son, Zachary, who was the spitting image of his dad. As we talked and ate, I learned that Renee loved to dance and her time was filled with lessons and recitals. And as with most teenage girls, she acted much older than she was.

Zachary enjoyed trading sports cards, wrestling, and basketball, with hopes of being in the NBA someday. We had a very pleasant time and I learned to enjoy my fries with ranch dressing instead of catsup, thanks to Renee. I was relieved the kids didn't ask me any awkward questions about my relationship with their dad and hopefully I would be seeing more of them in the near future.

"Oh Chanukah, Oh Chanukah
Come light the Menorah."

The holidays were here and I invited my sister to go to the mall and help me pick out a gift for my new boyfriend.

"I don't want to buy too much, Lori; after all, we just started dating," I told my sister.

"Knock it off, just keep looking," she demanded. I found a black suede vest and held it up and said, "Hey Lori, do you like this?"

"That's all you are buying?" she asked and resumed looking on the rack for more. *Why did I bring her anyway?* I ended up buying a few more things, hoping he wouldn't think I was being too forward.

Ari invited me to his parents for their family Chanukah party. I wanted to buy gifts for everyone. This was the first time I was going to meet the entire family, including his two eldest children from his first marriage.

Well, the holiday had arrived and I was more than a little nervous. Because he had to pick up the kids first, we made plans to meet at the multi-family colonial where his parents and sister lived. When I pulled up, Ari greeted me and helped me bring in some of the gifts. As I stepped in the door, he made the introductions. I met Ari's two older kids, Holly and Evan, and we enjoyed small talk for a brief time. And I gave Renee and Zachary a big hug, which was a nice start.

We had to make a couple of trips to my car to bring in the rest of the gifts, and it felt so wonderful to be around a family that showed so much love to one another. Once the gifts were unloaded, I joined his mom and sister in the kitchen where they were busy cooking the sizzling potato latkes, cheese blintzes, and all the trimmings.

Everything was so delicious, and it was wonderful to see the warm interactions of this family of thirteen people having a holiday together. Ari and I, sitting across from one another, couldn't help staring at times. I was having feelings that were unfamiliar to me. As we sat around the table eating, one by one Ari's children began talking about Ari's ex-girlfriends; one was too old, the other too young, one was too mean and the other too dependent. Without ever asking I had gotten a detailed rundown of my boyfriend's romantic past. Ari just sat and listened with a smirk on his face, never saying a word.

Following dinner, we moved into the living room and the kids were assigned the task of passing out the gifts. My heart was racing, and I was surprised to see a huge stack of gifts with my name on them. I felt like a kid in a candy store. As I un-wrapped my gifts, I made sure that I saved Ari's present for last. It was a huge box and I nodded to him for help. Ever so slowly I pulled it out. It was a beautiful, black ceramic figurine called 'Eternity'. It was a circular piece of a man and woman intertwined by their arms and legs. To look at it, you couldn't tell where the male ended or where the female began.

Ari seemed to enjoy his gifts and tried the vest on immediately. Everyone approved of it and we hugged and kissed, and our eyes seemed to lock in place.

"I will call you later to say goodnight," Ari assured me as I was saying my goodbyes to the family. The evening ended all too soon; as I walked out to my car I wept tears of joy. I knew in my heart that this is the way a family is supposed to be.

Ari and I were about to spend our first New Year's Eve together. He made reservations at a banquet hall open to the public. As soon as we walked in, I knew this would be an interesting evening, and, oh my G-d, was I nervous; I saw that the entertainment was none other than my old boyfriend, Max Stein.

I was so happy to be with Ari and found I had absolutely no feelings for Max when we exchanged pleasantries. As we approached our table, I stopped dead in my tracks again, when I ran into my first ex-husband Rob, with his fourth wife on his arm. Rob was very cordial and wished us well. No big *mitzseah* (no big deal). The evening was nerve-racking at first, but we ended up having a great time dancing, kissing, and being together. Ari made me feel like we were the only two people at the party and I will never forget it.

Time flew by as we continued to date each other, and before we knew it, it was Valentine's Day. This was the holiday for lovers, and for the first time in my life I had one for the holiday.

I planned on the ultimate romantic Valentine's Day dinner at my house. We began the evening with cocktails followed by a scrumptious dinner of steamed lobster with sautéed redskins. Ari gave me a sexy little black negligee and a balloon with the words 'I'm falling for you' printed on it. I bought him a box of Godiva chocolates and a lighthearted Valentine's Day card.

In the past we had always practiced safe sex, but this evening was different. As we intertwined in each other's arms making love, something felt different and I knew in my heart that I was going to be pregnant. However, I did nothing to stop it, allowing nature and our hungry bodies to carry me away.

A few weeks later, my period was late. I raced into the house with my package from the drugstore and followed the instructions to a tee. I waited, nervously.

"Positive," I said aloud thrilled out of my mind, as I looked at the EPT not at all surprised by the results. Being pregnant was something I'd always wanted but I was unsure how Ari would respond to my news. I looked at myself in the mirror and smiled, enjoying the idea of bringing a baby into the world and vowing in my heart that he or she would be loved, cared for and confident. I suddenly remembered, before meeting Ari and Dr. Kaplan, I had considered getting pregnant on my own and now here I was. I wasn't afraid to face a future as a single mom. However, I knew in my heart Ari wouldn't feel the same.

"Honey, I have some news for you," I said over dinner the next evening. Ari sipped his drink and smiled.

"You do? What about?" he asked in such an innocent loving way.

"I'm pregnant," I said letting out a sigh of relief and hiding my excitement. He stared at me without saying a word.

"But listen, you don't have to take any responsibility whatsoever. You don't have to marry me. If you want you can even stop seeing me right now," I said nervously, hoping he wouldn't take me up on my offer.

Then I went on to tell him that an abortion was not an option. He looked at me silently for what seemed like hours, sipped his drink, took a deep breath and said,

"Let's not make any decisions right now and we'll see what happens."

He gulped the last of his drink and the rest of our evening was quiet. Though I never ventured to ask what he meant by his comment, I did relish the idea of carrying a baby, Ari's baby. I secretly hoped it was a boy and considered all the things I would do during my pregnancy and once he was born. The only physical feeling I had was being dreadfully tired. I decided not to talk to him about all my new feelings because he was "waiting to see what happens," whatever that meant.

A stabbing pain in my stomach woke me from my sleep. I was eleven weeks pregnant and I raced to the bathroom and found that I was bleeding and called my sister, crying.

"Lori, I need to go to the hospital, something is wrong."

She came over a few minutes later and drove me to the emergency room.

"If you are having a miscarriage, than it wasn't meant to be," she said to comfort me as she drove to the hospital. I was crying harder now, more from the thought of losing my baby than from the pain. I now knew what he meant.

After a few hours in the hospital my attending doctor diagnosed that I had lost the baby. However, the strange thing was I never had a D&C (dilation and curettage). They sent me home and prescribed bed rest. It was Saturday night and I had plans with Ari to go see his daughter in a dance recital. I dialed his number and told him about the miscarriage.

"Just rest honey and I'll call you tomorrow." He sounded sad, but I knew without question he was relieved. He called first thing the next morning and I said,

"Ari, I'm still in so much pain and something doesn't feel right."

Within twenty minutes he was at my door. His concern for me felt wonderful and I knew it was genuine. He drove me back to the hospital and they took me in right away.

He said, "I'll be right here waiting for you." Even though there was no sign of life inside me, the fetus still lay inside me and the physician on staff enabled me to deliver my baby naturally as if I were having natural childbirth. I cried knowing that Lori had been right—it wasn't meant to be. Ari came in to see me and held me as I cried, smashing my face into his chest. After a few minutes he pulled away, tenderly touching and kissing my face.

"Honey, I need to go pick up my kids. Can you get a ride home?" he asked, and though his voice was tender, his words shocked me.

I couldn't believe he would leave me lying in a hospital bed after losing a baby, his baby. But just as fast as the thought came, I realized that being a devoted father to his children was one of the qualities that attracted me to him.

"Sure honey, go ahead," I lied to him and to myself. *How could he just leave me here alone considering what I just went through? This is crazy and it really hurts more than losing the baby. He can't handle this, what a jerk!* I called my sister to pick me up, and we sat in comfortable silence during the drive home.

Later that evening, he called and said, "I'm so sorry honey, I was in a daze. I was torn, thinking what if you did have the baby; I would be a father to five kids. I was scared and petrified. I was just screwed out of my life savings. I'm working two jobs and I can't get caught up."

"But wait a minute," I interrupted.

"Please honey, just listen. It was like I was regressing back to when I was eighteen. Then you lost the baby and I didn't know what to do either. I felt so sad for you. I'm so sorry I will never leave you again, no matter what. I really do love you."

"I feel depressed and I can't seem to let it go," I said.

153

"I'm so sorry. What can I do to make you feel better?" he asked sincerely.

"I don't know if I'll ever feel better. I wanted this baby more than anything. He was already a part of my life," I said, now with tears and sniffles.

"Sure you will over time. I promise you'll feel better, because I love you. Can I have a kiss?"

I forgave him, but I knew I would never forget. After a couple days of rest and a lot of apologies and flowers from Ari, all was forgiven.

I was back to reality and decided it would be best to get a different job after witnessing some un-ethical business practices from my previous builder. I did end up taking him to court and won. After only two weeks of searching, I was hired to represent a company from Chicago, Illinois. They had purchased a prestigious high-rise apartment complex in Southfield, Michigan and hired me to handle the conversion from apartment rentals to owner-occupied condominiums. The ironic part was Ari used to live in this building and knew a lot of my clients.

My new company had parties to entertain the current residents and persuade them into purchasing their units. Ari would attend these events with me and enjoyed socializing with everyone.

"I hope he does you as well as he does the room," one of my co-workers whispered in my ear.

I smiled widely and nodded. "He does me just fine." We both giggled.

I was still very happy in our relationship. But from time to time I thought about the baby I had lost and how he had abruptly left me lying all alone in the hospital bed without a ride home. I never told anyone else besides my sister that he left me there, but I knew one day I would ask him again, "Why? How could you?"

CHAPTER TWELVE

"Never Thought That I Could Love"

Dan Hill

After the miscarriage, Ari and I were closer than ever. Actually, we were inseparable, and when I looked at the eternity statue he gave me at Chanukah, I knew he had a place in my heart.

"Are you relieved or disappointed about my losing the baby?" I asked him during one of our tender moments.

"I feel a little of both," he said in all honesty and I believed him.

As time went on I noticed that Ari seemed happier and stronger. He seemed to have more confidence, was smiling more and he was much more attentive to me.

One evening as I was upstairs getting ready, I heard Ari come into the house. I yelled, "I'll be right down honey!"

While I was adding the final touch of lip gloss, I realized the sponge tip was stuck on my lower lip. Unexpectedly, I heard the most beautiful love song playing with the volume soaring through my house and body. With chills running up and down my spine, I froze in the moment.

"You are the dream that saved my life
You are the reason I survived."

I walked to the top of the staircase and looked down and saw him standing on the landing gazing up at me. I ran down the stairs with tears for this dreamy man and jumped into his open arms. I knew at that moment that I really loved him.

Ari began talking about going back into the deli business on his own. He didn't want a restaurant that was full service, to avoid the labor problems, so he planned on a carry-out deli.

June of 1996 marked nine months that we had been dating. It was the best and healthiest relationship I'd ever had.

He knew all the right buttons to push; I never felt more feminine and womanly. One evening after we had made passionate love, we were lying in one another's arms. It was around three in the morning and he was staring up at the ceiling.

"Do you want to get married?" he asked casually.

"Are you proposing to me?" I asked him, shocked by his question.

"Yes, I am," he assured me.

This was so unexpected; I had given up the thought of ever being married again.

"Can I ask you something first?" touching his hairy chest with my fingertips.

"Sure, Honey," he said twirling my messy hair between his fingers.

"Will you have just one more little baby with me?"

"Yes, when the time is right," he said, and I hugged him so tight and excitedly said, "Yes I will marry you."

"I love you," he said as we kissed and held each other close.

"I love you, too." I said back to him.

After a time of gentle lovemaking, we fell asleep in each other's arms. I woke up first and stared at Ari as he slept. I couldn't believe that this hunk of man was going to be my husband. *Oh my G-d, I'm getting married for the third time.* I wanted to get up and call Mom, Lori and Jennifer. Ari woke up a few minutes later while I was in deep thought about all that I had to do. He looked at me with a wide smile on his face.

"Honey, I have a lot of calls to make," I told him.

"I'm sure you do," he said closing his eyes for a little more sleep. I got up and grabbed a cup of coffee as I rushed to the phone. Everyone was happy when I announced the news, but I'm not sure about Jennifer. Mom was thrilled; Lori accepted her maid of honor part and Jen said with a touch of sadness, "Of course I'll be your bridesmaid, I'm never the bride. Maybe one day, Dori, you'll stand up for me at my wedding."

"I know I will," I answered.

Jen had been living with Marvin for a year now and I really didn't know what their plans were. I didn't believe in living together but apparently she did. *Oh how he's getting all that milk for free.* However, it sounded like she wanted more.

Over the next few weeks, Ari and I talked about setting the date.

"Honey, how does New Year's Eve sound? That would be a fun night to get married, what do you think?" I asked.

"That's a little soon; it's only six months away. We should wait a little longer, so we can have our very own special date, one that belongs to us."

"That's fine with me, my husband-to-be," I said with a smile, realizing the logic behind his words.

We both looked through the calendar. It was the middle of June 1996 and we wanted a date that neither of us had been married on before. We finally picked Sunday, May 25th, 1997. Even though it was eleven months away and a holiday weekend, it was a perfect time of year to get married for all the right reasons. He thought a long engagement was a good idea, and though I was hesitant at first, I agreed.

We mutually agreed to live apart until after we were married, then he would move into my condo. For now, I had a wedding to plan. *I could have been a wedding planner.* Ari continued to work on getting his carry-out deli up and running.

He put a deposit on a free-standing building for rent with his savings, and he borrowed a small amount of money to attain the funding that he needed. After signing the lease, adding some equipment and cleaning up the place, he was ready to open. The night before the opening we went out for Chinese food and he realized he had no cash on him.

"I just realized I'm broke. I have no money on me." He seemed shocked by this realization.

I gently touched his arm and said, "Honey, you're not broke, you just have no cash on hand, and I am so proud of you," kissing him on the cheek.

Without hesitation, I paid the bill. The next day, Gourmet Deli Inc. opened, and it was an immediate success.

Because Ari didn't like to owe money, he made paying back the loan a priority.

"Bridge Over Troubled Water."

As my life was on an upswing, both professionally and personally, my mom and Harry's life was changing in the opposite direction. They had moved from Phoenix to Southern Florida, but the bad economy had taken a horrible toll on their financial future.

Harry needed and desperately wanted a change, which confirmed my decision not to move to Phoenix. During my busy time, Mom called often, only this time she asked, "Dori darling, would you fly down to Florida, just for a few days to help us find a place to live? I know you have a lot going on, but I would really appreciate it."

"When tears are in your eyes,
I will dry them all."

She hoped as a real estate broker I could help find them something nice. It was a bittersweet trip, because a few months ago Harry had had a mini-stroke and had not been the same since. I spent the entire time taking Harry to his doctor appointments instead of helping them find a new home. The stroke turned out to be a reaction from his medications. However, after Harry was feeling better, they did manage to find a retirement community on their own.

Though my mom didn't like it there, they settled in anyway. Shortly thereafter, Harry began to distance himself from Lori and me because of depression over his failing health. I felt such a tremendous loss because he no longer spoke with me on the phone nor sent me his warm loving notes as he once had. It was heart wrenching to see a once lively man, whom we all loved, become depressed and ill. My trip was harder than I thought it would be.

I was so happy to be back home; it seemed like I had been gone longer than three days.

If putting my life on hold, just for a few days, made a difference in my mom's life, then I knew I did the right thing.

Ari and I decided to have our reception at our favorite café where we knew we would get great food and the best service. The owner promised us the best wedding party ever.

"Over the miles."

"I'm moving to Phoenix," Lori announced over lunch one bitter cold February afternoon. She went on to tell me that she and a few of her girlfriends were all moving out there together. I was shocked, but happy for her.

"Dori, I need a change and I want a new beginning," she said truthfully.

I'm sure you do, you've been through enough losses in one lifetime," I said in all honesty.

After suffering from her own trials and tribulations, maybe this is the right thing for her to do. Lori had become a strong spiritual woman who is

160

honorable and filled with gratitude. I trusted her and wouldn't think of questioning her judgment.

"Would you list my condo?" she asked as we enjoyed our dessert and sipped our coffee.

"Absolutely and I will give you the family discount too," I said, excited about her new move but at the same time feeling very sad over the distance that would inevitably separate us.

Her home had a great deal of equity built up and it sold immediately. Moving day came much too soon for me. I was surprised at how much I grieved over her leaving, and I cried for more than three weeks.

The wedding plans kept me very busy and worked well as a distraction from Lori's departure. I was working on the invitations and looking for the appropriate dress.

Ari and I planned the entire dinner menu which included appetizers, too. Then we began to examine our guest list when I hit a snag, Jennifer and escort. *What about her live in boyfriend, my second ex-husband Marv?* I wasn't comfortable inviting my ex-husband to my wedding as her guest. They had been living together for two years now, which was no surprise to me. Actually it made a lot of sense because they were so much alike.

Marv was no longer a part of my life and one thing for sure she had no part in our breakup, or anything to do with the problems of our marriage. She introduced us and that was it. Even though her lies devastated our indestructible friendship, love and patience from both sides allowed us to heal and rebuild. She was the one person in my life who never left me. Jen, not Marvin, mattered to me and always will. When we had spoken weeks before, she insisted I should invite Marv because she was living with him. Ari didn't seem to mind at all but it bothered me.

"Jennifer, I'll feel very uncomfortable if I invite him" I told her gently and with all sincerity. I held my breath during the brief silence on the end of the phone.

"If you were married to Marv, I would have to invite him. But inviting him just because he's your boyfriend doesn't sit right with me," I added as I bit my lip waiting for her response.

"Well, you shouldn't be uncomfortable, Dori, I'll be there with or without Marv." She agreed and my dilemma was over.

Garrett, my dear friend from Dallas, was coming in for the wedding and offered to be Jennifer's escort, which meant a lot to me so she wouldn't be alone.

Ari and I wanted a small sacred ceremony with only about fifty people in attendance. We thought this would be the most proper since it was the third marriage for both of us. I used the help of my lady friend who had designed our wedding invitations and helped me organize my wedding party. She planned the entire ceremony to perfection for me in black and white. I transcribed her scribbled notes into an outline and gave a copy to everyone involved.

Searching for the right dress was the fun part, so I took Ari's daughters on a shopping spree. I told them the color and they chose the style. As far as the men were concerned, it was simply black tuxedos and everyone was happy.

The hardest part was finding just the right gown for me. This was such an important event, and I wanted to be dressed appropriately, with a bit of sex appeal for Ari. My first wedding I was dressed like a princess, and in my second I was dressed like a bride from the twenties. After much searching I found the perfect ivory two piece gown. It was quite dramatic and very stunning, with a high slit up the leg.

When I went to the post office to mail out the invitations, my heart was pounding a mile a minute, and I felt as if I couldn't breathe. This was my third mailing, and it had to be the last. I was madly in love with Ari, and for the first time in my life I could visualize spending the rest of my life with him.

As we continued to make our plans, I really wanted my parents to give me away. This would be the first time my dad had any involvement in a major life event. Since he lived nearby, I thought even though he failed at connecting with us, he might want to do the fatherly duty of giving his daughter away. Both he and my mom agreed to participate in my wedding; I was thrilled. Even though my parents hadn't spoken to one another in many years, this selfless act of love meant a lot to me.

As I looked over my to-do list, I mentioned to Ari, "Honey, it's time for us to go look for wedding bands."

We had skipped over the engagement ring part, which was fine with me. The following week Ari and I went ring shopping. I really didn't see anything I liked because they all were so average looking; I wanted something special that really spoke about our love.

"Honey, why don't you go out looking on your own and when you find something you like, then I will come and see it," he said lovingly.

"All right, Honey, that works for me." I agreed and knew his time would be better spent at work anyway.

The ring I chose was a wide, white gold band filled with diamonds and two thin yellow gold bands on each side. The gold bands represented the circle of love, and the setting was absolutely beautiful.

A few days later, when Ari had some spare time, he met me at the jewelry store to see the setting. The salesman remembered me and brought out the setting and placed it on a black velvet tray for us.

"Is this what you want, Honey?" Ari asked with an approving smile.

"Yes, Honey, I really love it"

"That's all that matters," he said, hugging me.

Then, we found a gorgeous two-tone yellow and white gold band for Ari and the rings were ordered. He seemed just as happy as I was. Since everything with us was done in such a loving manner, we went right home and wildly expressed it.

Over dinner the next night Ari gave me another surprise.

"Honey, I picked out a sparkling one karat princess-cut loose stone for your engagement ring. But you'll have to pick out the setting," he announced. I was shocked by it, never even thinking about an engagement ring, we were way past that part. I squealed with joy and hugged him.

The following day after going through several jewelry stores, I found the perfect setting. The manager allowed me to take it home on approval to show Ari and he loved it too. I was elated. *Hi G-d, it's Dori. Thank you for sending this man to me.*

I didn't have the nerve to call Rabbi Stein who is a Reformed Rabbi to perform my third wedding ceremony. There are three forms of the Jewish religion that people practice: Reformed, Conservative and Orthodox, the most religious of all. Ari and I discussed having a Conservative ceremony instead of Reformed because there were a lot more blessings and traditions involved. With four failed marriages between us, we needed and wanted as many blessings as possible.

At the first of our two meetings with our new rabbi, he explained to us about all the different traditions he could perform, one of which is called an *Oof Ruff* (a special blessing). This traditional ceremony is done prior to the wedding, where the Rabbi recites special blessings to the couple with the immediate family and friends present. When the ceremony ends they throw candy at us as we stand on the *Bema* (the sacred alter) in celebration of our upcoming marriage. He also told us, according to Jewish tradition and in G-d's eyes Ari and I were still married to our ex-spouses because Ari's ex-wife Sheila and I had never gotten a *Get* (a traditional Jewish divorce).

"It is imperative that you do this right away," the rabbi demanded.

"I'll call my ex and ask her if she would take care of this minor detail," Ari responded.

We scheduled our next meeting and said our goodbyes. *I hope Sheila is willing to do this; I don't see why she wouldn't be. This is so nerve racking.*

A few days went by since finding out we couldn't get married unless this dilemma was resolved. As I was wondering if Sheila agreed to go through the *Get,* the phone rang. Checking the caller ID, I saw it was Sheila. *Oh no, why is she calling me?*

"Hello," I answered calmly.

"Hi Dori, it's me Sheila. Ari just called and explained your problem. I thought since both of us have to do this, why don't you make the appointment with the Rabbi and we could drive together."

I was shocked and didn't know how to respond. However, we had been on good terms and as long as she was willing to do this in order for Ari and me to be married, why not?

"That would be nice, let me call Ari, I'll call you right back," I responded quickly and immediately called my fiancé'.

"Guess what, Honey? Sheila just phoned and she's willing to see the rabbi, but she wants to drive together."

"Are you serious?" he asked, shocked too.

"Well, how do you feel about that?" I asked nervously.

"I guess fine, it needs to be done," as I heard a little laugh at the other end of the phone.

"OK Honey, that's all I needed to know, thank you and have a wonderful day, I love you."

"Love you, too." He reiterated.

As I hung up the phone, I was wondering what was going through his mind? He acted like it was no big *metsiyeh* (mitz-see-ya) (deal). I called her back and the plans were set for the next week. We also agreed that afterwards, maybe we would go out for breakfast and get to know each other a little better.

I picked her up the following Tuesday at 1:00pm sharp; the odd thing was I wasn't there to get her kids; I was picking up their mother instead. She got in the car and we had small talk most of the way there. We each had to have a private ceremony with the Rabbi, and it was all over in thirty minutes. We stopped for a bite to eat, since we both had some extra time. While we were eating, some people we both knew came up to the table to say hello and surprise was written all over their faces. Sheila and I just laughed it off.

"Dori, if you have any questions about Ari, feel free to ask me anything," she offered. She was kind to offer her advice, but I happily declined.

"You Dropped a Bomb on Me."

Four weeks before the wedding, we had our second and last meeting with the rabbi for premarital counseling. We had everything in place. A small party of fifty people would be attending the ceremony and wedding reception and more than ever, we were both very much in love with each other. Dr. Kaplan was right; I was having feelings that were not to be believed.

I met Ari in the rabbi's study at the synagogue; he stood up and greeted me with a kiss and we sat across from the rabbi. Both Ari and I were nervous. He began addressing some of the complexities that may affect us in our future life together. He also talked about honoring one another and being there for one another. Even though he knew about our multiple marriages, he spoke to us as if we were getting married for the first time, which I really appreciated. For the first time in my life, I listened to every word he said.

"Dori, do you want to have children?" the rabbi asked.

"Yes, Ari and I have discussed it and we both agreed to have one child, when the time is right," I said, looking over at Ari and squeezing his hand as if to confirm what he said at his proposal.

"Is this how you feel, too?" The rabbi asked Ari.

"No. I don't want anymore children," Ari said dryly, avoiding eye contact with me.

Oh my G-d, I feel like my heart is ripped in half and I want to run out of here right now. It was very difficult to keep my composure. My heart was pounding so hard, and I wanted to scream. *Why is he lying?*

"You look a little pale Dori. Would you like a glass of water?" the rabbi offered.

"No thanks, I'll be leaving in a minute." I said furiously.

My face must have lost all of its color because I wanted to puke.

"Why aren't you telling the truth?" I asked him. Without giving him a chance to answer I added, "When you proposed to me, before I said yes, my one question to you was, are you willing to have a baby with me?" And your answer was, 'Yes, when the time is right.' That was when I agreed to marry you!"

"I never said that." He defended himself by explaining that he already had four kids and wanted to enjoy the rest of his life alone with me.

"Then why didn't you say that from the beginning?" I asked him, wiping my eyes and sniffing back the tears. I was crushed and stood up to leave. I couldn't stand to look at him, and I wanted to run as far away as I could. *How can I marry a liar?* This is not the man I thought I was marrying. I was livid at this point and didn't care what else the rabbi had to say. I walked out and he followed in silence. Feeling crazed, I got into my car and sped away. His words, my words were echoing in my mind. The tape recorder in my head played back, *evaluate, evaluate, and evaluate.*

A few hours later, Ari came over as always. He had a pathetic look on his face, only this time I felt no pity for him. He paused, looked at me, and instead of asking, "Where do want to go for dinner tonight?" he asked, "Do you need time to think?"

"Yes, I do!" I said adamantly.

"I understand," he said cowardly, and left.

I lay on the couch and thought about what had just transpired between us.

"You turned me out, you turned me on
And then you dropped me to the ground."

"Without respect or trust you have no love." Rabbi Stein's words came to memory as I covered my head entirely with the afghan. I replayed it all over; how much we loved one another, how good we were for each other. But the trust that once existed was now dust blowing in the winds of tribulation.

Then, after a time of crying and analyzing, I thought about the idea of just being married to Ari without having a baby, and I realized that would be all right, too. However, the burning question of why he lied was digging into my heart, and I felt nauseated all over again. I was also wondering where he was, what he was doing, and what he was thinking. I knew I really loved him and I had a decision to make.

After I got into bed alone trying to fall asleep, my thoughts were still erratic; *should I or shouldn't I marry him, knowing he didn't want anymore children? What will happen if I backed out now? Would I be throwing away the best thing that has ever happened to me? What about the lie? Was this his first lie and will it be his last?* My questions seemed to scream out for answers yet the answers seemed to be evading me just as sleep had been all night long.

The next morning I woke up and made some coffee. Even though I didn't get much sleep, I was still uncertain about the betrayal, but I knew that I loved him. After sipping some coffee I picked up the phone and dialed his number.

"Hi, Honey, how are you?" he asked tiredly. It felt good to hear his voice.

"You sound awful, where are you?" I asked, hearing hoarseness in his voice and noise in the background.

"I'm in some hole-in-the wall diner, having breakfast without you." There was silence and then he added,

"I've been driving around most of the night, thinking about you and me."

"Would you like me to meet you, so we can talk?" I offered.

"Yeah, can you come right now?" he asked.

"I'm on my way," I said and hung up the phone.

I desperately needed to know why he lied to me, but more than that I needed to see the man who I was madly and passionately in love with. When I arrived, Ari looked *farmisht* (confused), defeated and drained.

"I'm so sorry I hurt you. It was a weak moment, when I agreed to have another baby. I wish I had met you thirty years ago and maybe my life would have been different."

"Do you think we would have made a beautiful child together?" I asked.

"F*** yea!" he said bluntly.

"Honey, I love you so much and all I want is to enjoy the second part of my life playing with you. I want to travel and see the world, not be stuck home changing diapers," he admitted.

"I understand, but promise you'll never lie to me again," I said.

"I promise honey. So will you still marry me?"

"I would be happy to spend the rest of my life as your wife, whether I'm the mother to your child or not."

We made up and embraced in a long hug. I didn't want to let go, thinking I might lose him, only this time it would be for good. After embracing and kissing, we both went off to work, knowing that our relationship would grow deeper with each passing day.

About a week later, Ari came over straight from work with Zachary who was joining us for dinner. They had stopped by the market and Zachary was carrying a paper bag filled with groceries.

"I'm starving, Dori, can you make me a salad?" Zachary asked. He loved his salads, so I took the bag from him and looked in it. Wedged between the lettuce and the tomatoes was a jewelry box. I looked at my boys and then slowly pulled out the box.

"What's this?" I asked as I opened it. My mouth hung open when I saw he had picked up our wedding rings. I ran to hug them both and we had a fun-loving dinner, while I tried to breathe normally. After we finished eating, Ari whispered in my ear, "Honey, I felt scared earlier, when I picked up the rings, but this confirmed I love you and I'm really getting married again."

"Honey, I'm nervous too," I confessed.

Our wedding was one week away and my future in-laws had given us a lovely engagement party in their home. We also had our *Oof Ruff* at the synagogue and the blessings had begun. It was a very special and beautiful ceremony. We stood front and center on the *Bema* (the sacred alter) and held each other. Following the ceremony, our guests threw the traditional candy. I felt so loved and honored, knowing deep down in my soul, for the first time in my life, this marriage was the real thing.

While stopped at a traffic light the following day, I began to get anxious once again and a thousand thoughts ran through my brain. *Should I get married again? How can I marry a liar? Why would he lie to me? What if he lies again and again and again?* Doubts were blazing like a forest fire in a windstorm and I began to cry. I grabbed my cell phone and thought about calling Dr. Kaplan for an emergency appointment and then abruptly stopped the car when I heard an answer coming from the radio.

"Call now for your free psychic reading." I pulled off the road and quickly dialed the number.

"This is Miss Nelson, may I help you?" She said in a low scary voice.

"Yes, I hope so," I blurted out and proceeded to explain everything in a manner of two minutes.

"Calm down and listen to me carefully," she said and then added the very words I didn't expect to hear,

"Do not marry this man, you will never be happy, he is not for you."

"What?" I said under my breath, and then thanked her for her time and quickly hung up.

Her painful words ripped through my heart. I took a deep breath and decided to ignore the entire episode.

As I calmed down and resumed my errand running, I realized the irony of Ari already having the four children I had always wanted. Even though I didn't give birth to them, we could still be one big happy family. I knew in my heart we were getting married for all the right reasons and no psychic could tell me otherwise. I deserved and wanted to be happy and I planned on spending the rest of my life with him.

CHAPTER THIRTEEN

"Grow Old With Me"

Mary Chapin Carpenter

Our wedding day finally arrived on Sunday, May 25th, 1997. We took the old fashion route and agreed not to see each other for at least twenty-four hours before the wedding. My sister Lori spent the entire day helping me with my hair, make-up, and all the finishing touches. I was a nervous wreck and she, like always, was a wonderful maid of honor. We had fun reminiscing and giggling like typical sisters.

We arrived at the synagogue early, and I had a few visitors in the bridal room as Lori helped me get into my gown. My almost stepdaughter, Renee, came into the bridal room with her girlfriend and told me they had written a speech and wanted to read it at the reception.

"Of course, Honey, that is so sweet and I'm very flattered," I told her and gave her a quick bear hug. Then Jennifer came in for a private moment of hugs and kisses and let me know she was there with Garrett as planned. Marv's name was never mentioned. Since we didn't have a rehearsal dinner, everyone in the wedding party received a typed out instruction sheet. The ceremony was less than an hour away, and the rabbi requested all of us meet in his study. Ari waited in the hallway while I entered the study because I didn't want my husband-to-be to see me until it was time. The rabbi performed a *bedecking* on me, which means he covered my face with the veil, while reciting more blessings.

Separately, Ari and I signed the *Kethubah* (Jewish marriage license). This is a very special document which explains the responsibilities of the bride and groom to each other. During this time in the rabbi's study, I began to look around to see who was there by my side. As I glanced over to the door, there stood my stepfather Harry, but Mom and Lori were nowhere to be found. My future mother-in-law and father-in-law, sister in-law and Ari's oldest son were there too. I looked up at the clock; it was five minutes before the ceremony.

"Come on, Dori, it's time to go," Harry said warmly as he took my shaking arm.

"Two branches of one tree."

He walked me down the hallway toward the small chapel where the service was about to begin. I took a deep nervous breath, but I knew even if I wanted to, there was no turning back now. I peeked through the door of the chapel and watched my wedding party as they walked in ahead of me. I noticed how everyone looked amazingly beautiful, especially the groom. As the intensity of the music grew, I entered the chapel, trembling, hoping no one noticed. *Well Dori, this is it.* I glanced around and saw the man of my dreams standing in front of the *Chupeh* (bridal canopy). Part of me wanted to run straight toward him, but I held myself back.

As I walked down the aisle on the white satin runner, I quickly scanned the chapel and saw my friends and family members smiling and *farclempt (choked up)* as I passed by them. My mom and dad walked toward me and she lifted my veil. They both kissed me on my cheeks. I couldn't believe my parents were together for me. Then mom gently lowered the veil back on my face and they both walked me arm in arm toward the center of the aisle. As was tradition, I stood and waited for Ari to come and get me. I held my breath, puzzled. Ari wasn't moving toward me. The music continued to play and it was obvious he didn't know what to do. He hadn't read my printout with all the specifics. Thankfully the rabbi spoke up, "Go get your bride!" Watching him nod, I breathed a sigh of relief as Ari walked towards me and gently placed my arm in his. And together we took our places under the *Chupeh,* hopefully for the very last time, where we became husband and wife.

Immediately following the ceremony, the rabbi took us into a private room for one solitary moment alone as husband and wife to solidify that we were now one, which is another Jewish tradition. Then we joined the rest of the wedding party at the café for our celebration filled with love, food, dancing and laughter.

When Ari and I walked into our party arm in arm, the room screamed of elegance. Each table was draped in crisp, white linen table cloths. The centerpieces included beautiful fragrant roses, illuminated by white candles flickering to the beat of our hearts. The room was filled with everyone we loved, and I was overflowing with feelings of enthusiasm for my husband, knowing I had finally made the right choice.

During the party the band played *Hava Nagila* and I was seated in a chair, holding on for dear life. Some of the men lifted me up and held me in the air while dancing in circles. While I was high in the air, I looked down and saw my dad sitting at his table. I waved and yelled,

"Hi Daddy," as if to say, "Look at me."
They were words I never had the chance to say before. Afterwards, I sat on his lap for a photograph and we did have one dance together. It was the first time I had ever danced with him, and it was a very special moment for me.

It was close to midnight when our last guest was leaving. Ari and I gathered our belongings and left for our wedding night. Since we were waiting until December to go on our honeymoon, we reserved a beautiful bridal suite at a nearby hotel.

We checked in as Mr. and Mrs. Ari Winger. Flowers and a bottle of champagne awaited us on the table in our suite, and it was very romantic. We sat on the bed and toasted to our new life together. Still euphoric from the wedding, sleep certainly wasn't on our minds. I had bought a beautiful sexy outfit, perfect for my wedding night. The lacy push up bra helped "the girls" look perky and firm. The matching French-cut panties enhanced my *tushy* (fanny) and the cover up was a feminine sheer flowing top with bell sleeves.

It was the color of a juicy peach, perfect to whet my husband's appetite.

"The best is yet to be."

It was my goal to remain the woman he fell in love with and not let myself change into someone he doesn't know. In my heart, I knew my love for him would grow deeper every day and this time, my husband shall be my first priority. *Wow, have I changed or what?* The sexy lingerie was not on too long before our magical evening of passionate lovemaking began. Afterwards, as I lay in his strong masculine arms, my mind wandered back to another place and time when I was unable to be sexually spontaneous or express my feelings without limitations.

"Honey, where are you?" he asked, as he saw I had mentally drifted away.

"I'm right here with you, Honey."

He kissed me tenderly, while touching my face and said, "I want to make a deal with you."

"OK, I love good deals."

"As my wife you can cook in the bedroom, but not in the kitchen."

"Sounds great, I can handle that."

It's a good thing our favorite restaurants are on speed dial because I'd rather have him for dinner anyway. As our bodies intertwined he gently kissed me all over until we finally fell asleep.

After returning to my condo, Ari had arranged to move his things in on the following Sunday. We decided to live there indefinitely until we found our dream home. A couple of days before the actual move, I helped him filter through his entire apartment. I was going through his closet and found an odd-looking shirt. I didn't want to come out and say it was old and worn looking, so I tried to handle it more gently. "Hey honey, do you want to look like this?" "No, that can be tossed," he replied. This was how my mom helped me clean out my closet and it worked great, without her saying it's ugly, get rid of it. If he said yes, he liked it, then it would be packed; if no then it was donated. The move, though hectic, went well and we settled into a new routine. We met with Ari's CPA, who helped join us financially as husband and wife. I even changed our answering machine message to reflect our new life together: "You have reached the Newlyweds."

A few months later friends of ours invited us out for a Fourth of July getaway on their yacht in Grand Haven, Michigan. This would be our first vacation together.

The weekend was great; we relaxed on the boat, sunning ourselves, and eating. We listened to great music and partied all weekend. At night we watched the most beautiful sparkling display of fireworks. We had an enjoyable ride home the following day.

As the new week began, I realized suddenly I had two new roles in life, being a wife and a step-mom. With that in mind, one day after work I went straight to the local bookstore to find a book on step-parenting.

After educating myself by reading and listening to radio talk shows, I learned it was not my place to discipline or tell the kids what to do. I also learned divorced fathers are filled with guilt so they overcompensate. With all my wonderful newly acquired knowledge about children, parenting, and step-parenting, I knew it would help me be a better friend and step-mom. If nothing else, I wanted to be a strong source of support and encouragement for my husband as he raised his children.

The following Saturday, Jen and I made our typical plans to spend the day s*hpotzing* (shopping). We never went out for lunch because she can't waste valuable time eating. We were in the tiny dressing room and I was zipping up a fabulous pair of jeans. I almost pinched my skin when she said excitedly, "Dori, I have a news flash! Marvin and I are engaged and we are going to be married next March."

"What did you say?" I asked.

Is this really happening? Oh my G-d! My best friend, who's been like a sister to me for twenty-five long years, is really going to marry my second ex-husband.

"Yes, it's true! Isn't it great?" She was happily chatting away.

"Oh my G-d Jen, I knew this was possible but now that it's a reality, I'm not sure how I feel. Believe me I want you to be happy, but come on, isn't this bizarre?" I asked.

"It's no big deal, it happens all the time to a lot of people," Jen reassured me.

"Yeah right, nothing is ever a big deal with you," I responded.

"Are you ok with this? I didn't want to tell you until it was official," Jen asked.

"Marv was never an issue with me since our divorce, but at least I thought he'd be out of my life for good. And now that's about to change because you—my best friend and matchmaker—are about to marry him."

"I know what you're saying and it is a little weird how it all worked out. But maybe one day we can all be friends and double date. We've never done that before, what do you think, girlfriend?" She asked in a fun-loving way.

"You're crazy; that will never happen!" I assured her. *Who knew?*

"Are you getting those jeans?" Jen asked.

"Get me out of this dressing room, I'm *shvitzing* (sweating) my guts out."

As we continued to walk the mall and window shop I said to her, "Listen, if Marv makes you happy, I'm ok with it. Oh Jen, *Mazel Tov!* I'm thrilled for you. Now it's your turn to have the traditional wedding you have always wanted. You'll be the beautiful bride walking down the aisle to your favorite love song," I said, feeling honestly happy for her, recalling her hopes and dreams.

"No, that won't be happening. Marv's dad is terminally ill, so we're going to Vegas with just our immediate families. We don't want to wait too long, especially if we want his dad at the wedding. The worst part is, Dori, you won't be there to stand up for me for a change," she added.

Jennifer tried to sound positive, but I detected a hint of disappointment in her voice. I loved her and would have been happy to be her maid of honor. But on the other hand I was relieved I didn't have to attend since it would have been awkward for everyone.

Jennifer called the next day to let me know they set the date for March 14th, 1998. They would have just the ceremony, Vegas style, and the following October they planned for a lavish reception in Detroit for family and friends to attend.

"But you know, Dori, I would love a real bridal shower," she said with a sigh.

"Why, Jennifer? You'll just return the gifts like you always do. Why do you want a shower anyway?" I asked.

"This is my first wedding and I want a bridal shower, just like everyone else!" She then added, "Why don't you have one for me?"

"Right, Jen, I'm your future husband's ex-wife. There is no way. But, I have a better idea. I can go in on the shower and share the expenses with the other girls. I'm sure they would love to give you a shower. How does that sound to you?"

"Oh, thanks Dori you're the best," she said as we hung up the phone.

I thought about our friendship over the years and about the problem we had when Marv and I were going through our divorce. I thought about the loss of trust I felt. However, I wanted her to be in my life because I loved her like a sister.

The fall season was approaching and the autumn colors brought with them plans for our long-awaited, but not forgotten honeymoon. Ari owned a time-share for two weeks in Cancun, Mexico. He always enjoyed his times there, but I was hesitant about going there for our honeymoon because he had shared it with many other women before me. I didn't want memory lane to interfere with our honeymoon. I thought that in some way it would take away from the purity of our relationship. But after much thought I realized that our relationship was much stronger then any memory.

It was a freezing, icy Michigan morning, but we made our way to the airport. We got up to the check-in counter and presented our papers to the clerk.

"Mrs. Winger, this is the wrong birth certificate," she said handing the paper back to me.

"What? That is my birth certificate." I said, dumbfounded by her comment.

"This is just a copy of your birth certificate. We need the one with a raised seal on it," she explained.

Ari and I looked at each other in horror. I began to cry.

"But this is our honeymoon and those little foot prints on that paper belong to me," I cried, while Ari held me close.

"Let me get the supervisor, one moment please," she said feeling slightly embarrassed. My internal panic button was going off like a siren on a police car. *Please G-d let us board the plane.* Moments later the supervisor appeared and smiled widely.

"We are going to let you through this time, however Mrs. Winger, it would be in your best interest to have the correct birth certificate," she said handing us our boarding passes. With a huge sigh of relief, we both thanked her and hurriedly left for the departure gate.

We arrived at a beautiful five star resort in Cancun, Mexico. It was early afternoon when we entered the two-bedroom condominium overlooking the glistening blue Caribbean ocean aligned with the cool white sand made out of limestone. I walked out on the balcony to see the radiant sunshine and the breathtaking view. Ari joined me on the balcony and announced, "Honey, this is all brand new furniture in the condo. They have redone the entire unit, so this is all fresh for me, too." *New furnishings, new memories, that works for me.*

The first morning of our honeymoon, I woke up and made a pot of coffee from the fresh ground Colombian he had brought from the deli. I grabbed a cup and my cigarettes and went outside to sit on the wraparound balcony. I looked at the endless miles of ocean, as the sun reflected on the ever-moving waves.

My mind wandered to thoughts of the movie *On a Clear Day You Can See Forever* and I stood up and began singing the title song of the film, not caring who heard me. I felt as if I could, indeed, see forever and my future had never been brighter.

Ari took me to all of his favorite restaurants, and we swam and played in the pool everyday. It was very romantic as he carried my weightless, floating body in his arms while he tenderly kissed my lips. When we tired of the pool, we went to the beach and held each other as the rushing waves beat against us. Then in the quiet of the evening surf we walked along the beach, hand in hand.

Later that evening, he took me to his most favorite restaurant, a beautiful Italian place, for dinner. Our table wasn't ready, so we went to the bar and ordered cocktails. As we stood, because there were no seats available, he raised his glass in a toast; a nice looking man seated next to us offered me his seat.

"No thank you, I'm fine."

"Please take my seat next to my lovely wife." He insisted and I accepted, realizing that chivalry was not dead. We introduced ourselves to one another. Their names were Lynn and Mickey, and we exchanged a few pleasantries before their table was called.

After dinner we went back to our condo and made love, as we did every day. He made me feel as if I was the most beautiful and loved woman in the world. He seemed to be waking up every womanly part of my body. As our hands and mouths began to explore one another, he moved on top of me, tasting every inch of my quivering moist body and then he entered me slowly and began thrusting until we had reached the summit of our mountain of love.

The next morning, we had a beautiful buffet breakfast at the resort. Afterwards, Ari went to pick up our towels while I went to find our lounge chairs by the pool for a day of fun in the sun. I found a couple of empty chairs right next to Mickey and Lynn, our new friends from last night.

We were all so excited to see each other once again. Not only did we connect the lounge chairs, we spent the entire day together. We learned they were from the Detroit area as well and we spent the rest of our vacation with them. At the end of the week, we made tentative plans to meet for dinner when we got back home and said our goodbyes. It had been a delicious honeymoon, without a doubt.

CHAPTER FOURTEEN

"We are Family"

Sister Sledge

During our first year of marriage, Ari's children had truly become an extended family to me. We decided to go back to Cancun and take the kids for a family vacation, which would give me a chance to get to know my stepchildren.

"Baby, I'm really nervous," I told Ari

"Don't be; you'll do just fine," he said.

"That's easy for you to say."

"My kids are going to love you," he said lovingly.

Holly is Ari's eldest daughter from his first marriage. She was in her early twenties, tall, thin, brown straight hair with a few blonde highlights framing her beautiful face. She has a great sense of humor and is fun to be with. She has a great job working for a local commercial tycoon and is constantly getting promoted.

Evan, Ari's eldest son also from his first marriage, was in his late twenties. He is tall, handsome and has a very strong physique. His bear hugs are amazing. His dynamite personality allows him to often win "Salesperson of the Month" selling shoes. On a Saturday, I took Jen with me to see Evan and maybe buy a pair of shoes. When we walked in he gave each of us one of his huge bear hugs.

"Just tell me your size Dori." He demanded.

"I'm a 9 medium. Don't rush, Evan I'm not going anywhere."

He raced through the store searching for just the right styles. He must have brought out a dozen shoe boxes and piled them up in front of me.

"You're like Prince Charming, slipping these shoes on and off my feet." We had the best time, and even Jen bought a pair. Three pairs later and the best deal I've ever had, it was time to go. Sadly, Evan could not join us on our family vacation due to his work demands.

Ari's youngest daughter Renee, from his second marriage, was in her early teens. She has been involved in tap, jazz, and ballet most of her young life. She is a fair skinned beauty with long curly hair and a strong lean body. With her endless energy, I knew she would keep us all entertained. I believe she had the hardest time with her father's new life. She was always daddy's little girl; however, after we were married, she began to distance herself. Renee told me since she was a little girl, she was always the one who took care of everything for him, especially with her baby brother. On their weekends with dad, she would help him with feedings and diaper changes. Now he had a new wife and she felt out of place.

When my parents divorced I remembered how torn up I was. During that time, I had a deeper need to be friends with the moms and dads of my girlfriends, rather than just the girls. I always wished my parents would get back together, which I'm sure Renee hoped as well.

Zachary, Ari's youngest son, was eleven years old. He was so cute and full of life. He had dark thick hair, dark brown eyes and a smile that reached from ear to ear. For a little guy, he displayed a gigantic personality and never got lost in the shuffle. He kept us busy with all his boundless energy and his hunger for ping-pong and water sports. He had a lot of friends back home which kept me busy carpooling. This was a new experience for me, and I loved it. I remember one day he called me from the movie theatre.

"Hi, Dori, would you pick me and my friend up, his mom can't come and get us?" he asked sweetly.

"Sure, Zach, I'll be right there."

I drove my little two seat black Toyota Celica and when I arrived, four boys piled in. Zach thought this was funny and so much fun. Thank G-d I didn't get stopped by the police; that wouldn't have looked good on my step-mom résumé.

*"We are family
Get up everybody and sing."*

Every day was fantastic and everyone was getting along. The sun was shining down on us and it was around 80 degrees. We ate breakfast together and spent our days at the beach and the pool. Holly and Renee spent their nights at the clubs and Zach was with us. One night it was about two in the morning and the phone rang. In my typical dead to the world sleep, I picked up the phone and then immediately hung it back up. Then it rang again; it was Holly.

"Dori, don't hang up, it's Holly. We're locked out!"

"I'm so sorry honey, I'll be right there."

After we arrived back from our family vacation, I had a new connection with my stepchildren, adding richness to my life.

Ari and I hosted our first Chanukah party for the family with gifts piled up in beautiful shining silver paper. It was crowded but cozy in our small living room, and I loved every minute of it.

Holly was the first one to approach me since our trip and said, "It was so nice getting to know you a little better. To be honest I was very nervous to spend a whole week with you. Why don't we go out for lunch sometime; maybe Renee could come too?"

"I would love that, anytime," I said.

Later on, Renee expressed her feelings too.

"Dori, let's go on a family vacation every year; I had so much fun."

"Sounds great, Baby Girl," I responded.

We were all glad Evan could make it, and he brought hugs and shoes for everyone.

As a child, I never had the opportunity to enjoy the warmth and closeness of family celebrations, so these times with Ari's family had become some of the most precious times of my life. As I watched everyone enjoying the traditional Jewish meal, my thoughts began to drift back to my childhood.

"Dori, what do you want do when you grow up?" Mom would ask me.

189

"Oh Mom, you know what I want. I want to get married to a nice man, have four kids, a big house with a fenced in backyard, and a dog." After forty years, I had obtained my dream life, though not quite the way I had envisioned doing it.

As the New Year arrived, our life was going well and moving forward. The deli was a huge success, so my brilliant husband decided he wanted to purchase the building for the deli because paying rent was a waste of money. Fortunately, Ari had a built-in real estate broker right at home and I was able to handle the entire transaction. He quickly contacted the landlord and we made an offer to purchase this little hole-in-the-wall freestanding building, which to us represented a gold mine.

We applied for a loan with a small bank and were approved immediately. A few months later, after we closed on the property, we received a letter of intent from a national drug store chain. They wanted to purchase our property, demolish our store and build a well-known drugstore. They were a very solid buyer, and we were thrilled out of our minds.

While Ari and I were sitting at the kitchen table mulling over this letter of intent, we realized we were in the unique position of selling our newly purchased property for a substantial amount of money. After about six months of negotiations, they gave us an offer we couldn't turn down. It would take about a year to close on the property, but we didn't care. During this time, Ari found another free-standing building to relocate the deli.

We were well into the new year when Ari found a second deli location. After we signed the paperwork, he opened the doors of our second deli on the same day as Jennifer and Marv's Vegas style wedding.

In a matter of weeks, it was a success too. I helped my husband often at the deli, being the one and only cashier at times. I really enjoyed being there, not only giving him wifely support, but for the employees as well. I often acted as a buffer between them and Ari, who once in a while would lose his cool when he was stressed.

Watching him in action, he was a bear. *Is that my husband screaming like that?* But I enjoyed servicing the customers and handling the negotiations as well. The more involved I got in our deli business, the less real estate I did. Though my career had taken a backseat, I kept my company and license active. I was content helping him and I no longer felt I had anything to prove to myself or anyone else for that matter.

Years earlier I would not have felt as comfortable letting my career go. As the deli businesses were picking up, I wanted to be available to support him anytime he needed it. "Honey, call me at 911-THE WIFE anytime," I would tell him when he left for work.

We were very happy together; our love relationship was growing deeper everyday without effort, and I loved how he loved me. When we would get into bed or on the couch at night to relax and watch television, he would always take my hand and melt it into his for the entire evening.

We knew in the back of our minds that someday in the future we would start looking for a new home of our own. However, in my mind it was more the distant future then the near future. The equity in my condo was the first and only financial security I had ever known. After two failed marriages, I wanted to be absolutely sure my marriage was rock solid and here to stay. I remembered Dr. Kaplan's words, *"You must evaluate."* Only this evaluation was going to take some time, because I refused to screw up my life again.

"Rock Around The Clock."

Ari was turning fifty, so I planned a surprise party for him about a week before his birthday. I found a fabulous fifties-themed restaurant and invited about sixty people. Even my mom came in from Florida for the big event. She couldn't stop *kvelling* (beaming) and bragging about her happily married daughter, something very rare in my family.

My husband had no idea what he was headed for when we walked into the restaurant with the kids. Renee and Zachary helped me pull the actual surprise off in a big way. The party was on a Sunday night, and we acted like we were just going out for a family dinner as usual. The only difference was we were going somewhere new for dinner and meeting a couple of friends.

When we arrived, he was busy pointing out the classic cars that were on display outside the restaurant to Zachary. As we walked in, I nodded to the kids to let their dad walk in first and the startled look on his face said it all.

"We're gonna rock, rock, rock, 'till broad daylight."

"SURPRISE!" Everyone yelled as the cameras flashed like an erratic sky lit up from bolts of lightening. He had a smile from ear to ear. He grabbed me and kissed me hard and the party was on.

Some of the female guests were dressed up in poodle skirts, leather jackets, and even Ari's father and brother-in-law were dressed like the Blues Brothers.

Fifties music was blaring and everyone was dancing and having a great time. I received many kind words of gratitude for a long time after the party was over, especially from Ari.

A few days later, Jennifer called me from Vegas following her wedding to Marv. She was in high spirits and I was happy for her. I did look forward to their wedding party in October with my husband by my side.

We celebrated my first Mother's Day ever with the kids. It was filled with sweetness; later we shared the holiday with my mother in-law and sister in-law, too. I read the card that Ari had given me, which was attached to a diamond tennis bracelet. *"Thanks for being so good to my children."* I was shocked; I never expected a gift on Mother's Day from him or anyone else, except perhaps my dog, Prince. Renee and Zachary bought me a beautiful card, which took me by surprise too, and I decided to keep it forever. Both Holly and Evan sent me a musical Mother's Day card through e-mail, which meant so much, as well.

Our first anniversary arrived. It still felt as if we were on our honeymoon, and we planned to remain newlyweds for a long time to come. We went out for a romantic dinner to our favorite café. As we lifted our glasses in a toast to our marriage, we stared into one another's eyes with great intensity.

"To my beautiful wife, thank you for giving me my life back," he said with tears in his eyes. I stood up walked over to him and kissed him tenderly.

After dinner, we came home and I reenacted our honeymoon, complete with my peach lingerie that I wore on my wedding night. This would become my anniversary tradition, as long as the outfit still fit. After we made love, we watched the video of our wedding and laughed at the petrified look on Ari's face.

"Baby, look how scared I was. I would have made the biggest mistake of my life if I wouldn't have married you," he said and I kissed him gently on the mouth.

"I love you, too."

Even after Jennifer's marriage to Marv, she and I were just as close. Though now when I wanted to speak to her, I only called her on her cell phone because I was still uncomfortable calling her at home. I realized I couldn't call her anytime I wanted, so I bought her a pager for her birthday.

Since she had already gotten married, we were holding her wedding shower after the fact. On this particular Saturday, one week before her bridal shower, we went *shoptzing* (shopping) for a change.

"Dori, I can't wait for my wedding shower, I'm especially excited to open all my gifts," she said as we ate lunch in the food court near one of her favorite department stores.

"Jennifer, don't forget I'm not going with you to return your gifts!" I assured her, and we both laughed.

"Dori, at my shower should I have someone make a ribbon bouquet on a paper plate?"

"You've got to be kidding me, grow up will ya?" I said shocked at the thought of it.

"I am!" she said with a laugh.

We enjoyed the rest of our day together, and then went home to our husbands.

"Sixteen going on seventeen."

194

Renee's sixteenth birthday arrived, and all she wanted was a purple car. However, even living in the motor city, this was not an easy find. But being the tenacious man that her dad is, he found just the right car for her.

It was so much fun to see him buying this car for his daughter. He was elated that he could afford to do it, since just a short time earlier, it wouldn't have been possible. Ari made sure her new car was sitting in the driveway when she came home to her mother's house, complete with purple balloons to match.

"I am sixteen going on seventeen
Innocent as a rose."

After Renee received her car, we noticed a gradual change in her behavior as she began to distance herself once again. She eventually stopped calling her dad and no longer spent the night at our house. She was out of our lives, always on the run, working or busy with her friends. This hurt Ari deeply. They had always been close, and he couldn't understand what was happening to their relationship. Her attitude toward him grew worse each day. At times, his fun-loving relationship with Zachary would be affected as well, and neither one of us understood why.

Renee had always been the center of his universe and he never missed a single dance recital. He loved his little girl, and couldn't identify with the distance she placed between them. Even though her attitude grew worse, she called her dad anyway to tell him she had a ticket for him for her next performance, but she did not mention having one for me. The next day, I stopped in to see him at work and he explained the earlier phone call from his daughter.

"Honey, I think I will go to see her perform, even though I haven't heard from her in weeks. I will come home immediately after her performance and not stay and talk with her like I usually do." *Oh my G-d, I have brain pain.*

"Honey, I'm not going to tell you what to do. However, if you go tonight, you will be condoning her bad behavior. This shows her that her recent actions toward you are acceptable and that it's okay not to acknowledge me as your wife," I said.

Ari was visibly torn by the situation, so I took his hand in mine and said, "Respect is earned, not a given, and right now she's being disrespectful to both of us. If you don't go to the recital, I realize this would be the hardest thing you have ever done. But you will send a huge message and break her rage. And hopefully, she will come back to you, her daddy."

We kissed good-bye and I left the deli knowing he was filled with regret over the way their relationship had dissolved. I hoped my advice was right because I didn't want to cause him any more emotional pain. Ari came home around five, clearly depressed about the situation and said in a depressing voice, "I called Renee and told her that I wasn't going to be at her recital. And a few minutes later my ex-wife gave me a malicious phone call and hung up on me."

I was proud of how strong he was and that he had stood his ground, but my heart ached for him. The following day, it seemed like my advice to Ari was right on. He called me from the deli with enormous news.

"Honey, you were right, Renee left me a voice mail last night after the recital. She was crying and yelling at the same time asking why I wasn't at her recital. I saved the message for you to hear later," Ari said in a voice of relief.

"Honey, why don't you invite her out for a fancy dinner, just the two of you and keep calling her until she accepts?"

Over the next few days Ari called her on three different occasions until she said yes. Everything went well, they talked things out and all was forgiven, he assured me without sharing the details. He did mention, "Renee said, she will call and apologize to you, too." However, I knew in my heart that wasn't happening. *What if I was dead wrong, telling Ari how to handle his daughter? But the important part was, he did break her rage and now their relationship had a chance to rebuild. Unfortunately, we still don't know what caused her to stay away.*

A few weeks later we celebrated Father's Day at my sister-in-law's house. There was a little tension between Renee and me, but I tried not to let it show. After dinner Renee placed her arms around me, hoping for a mutual hug, but I didn't return the gesture. When she realized that I wasn't going to hug her back, she walked off in a huff. Ari watched the entire scene, and this upset him to the point of leaving the room and I followed him.

"Honey, what's wrong now?" I asked him, bewildered by his disapproval.

"My wife and daughter are not speaking," he said in a frustrated tone.

"Please don't make it worse than it already is," I said firmly.

About an hour later, we were all sitting around the family room watching a video and I looked directly at Renee. *Well, she did make an attempt and I was the one who was being a child about it. I determined the situation had to change.*

"Renee, do you want to go outside and talk?" I asked her gently.

She looked at me and nodded. We sat on the patio and each lit up a cigarette. I tried to be as tender and diplomatic as possible, choosing my words carefully.

"When you hurt your dad, you hurt me too. And when you hurt me, you hurt your dad. His happiness is what matters to me. So can you please tell me what is going on with you?" I asked her and waited as she sighed.

"I feel like a stranger to you guys, and I don't have my dad in my life anymore!"

"Do you remember when you received your car for your birthday and you had your first taste of independence?"

"Yeah," she answered.

"Well you slowly distanced yourself from us with no more sleepovers with your girlfriends or Sundays at our house for brunch. I understand why you feel like you have lost part of your dad and maybe a little jealousy exists. I would have felt the same way if I was close to my dad and he remarried, but please understand that your dad has a new life now, and is finally a very happy man. The thing you must not forget, you are a part of our new life if you want to be."

"But Dori, I was the one that always took care of him," she said wiping away a tear.

"Would you rather have your dad be happy or sad?" I asked.

"Happy," she answered without hesitation.

"Your dad loves you very much and you mean everything to him. What do we need to do to make this situation better?" I asked, unsure of her response.

"I want to get to know you and dad again and be part of your lives," she said through her tears. Feeling *farclempt* (choked up) I stood up and gave her a big well-deserved hug and a kiss, and she reciprocated.

"I love you, Baby Girl."

"I love you, too," she replied and we went back into the house arm in arm.

Ari watched us walk in, and his huge smile showed a complete sense of relief.

"Everything is fine honey," I told him as I kissed his delicious lips.

As he drove us home, we sat in comfortable silence listening to the radio. *Maybe this is the reason I never had any children of my own, because G-d already had four ready-made kids waiting for me to love, share my life lessons, and be their friend.*

CHAPTER FIFTEEN

"Celebration"

Kool and the Gang

We had a beautiful wedding shower for Jen. While everyone was mingling, she pulled me to the side and said, "Dori, why don't the four of us double date?"

"No way, Jennifer! You're crazy. I can't be friends with my ex-husband. Why would you want that anyway?" I asked.

"It could be fun," she suggested.

"No way; end of story," I said.

She received a lot of beautiful gifts, but I opted to be practical and bought her a one-year subscription to *The Jewish News*. She wasn't too thrilled with my gift at the time, mainly because she couldn't return it. She enjoyed reading about our people, but never let me hear the end of it.

The next event was her wedding reception party. Since she and Marv had run off and done the Vegas thing, she wanted a lavish, fun-filled evening of eating, drinking, and dancing to celebrate their marriage with 150 of her closest family members and friends. After weeks of nerve racking planning, the evening had arrived.

"Stay close to me, Honey." I whispered in Ari's ear as we entered the celebration.

I had been feeling a bit anxious to be around Marv and my ex *mechutonim* (in-laws). To my surprise, they welcomed me with open arms and hugs. My former mother-in-law actually requested a picture with me. His entire family understood that I had not been at fault and Marv had clearly been the wrong man for me.

Jennifer looked beautiful and did a superb job, considering she had never entertained before. The evening had been going along perfectly, until I felt tension from her.

"I don't want her in the picture!" Jennifer yelled at the photographer when I joined the girls as they posed for a group picture. I couldn't help staring her down, stunned by her behavior. Apparently, when she saw the look on my face she changed her mind and invited me back in for the group picture. Her cold, harsh conduct continued throughout the evening, and I was disgusted by her ugliness. I was also in a daze because I didn't know why she was treating me this way. *Maybe she's having a nervous breakdown.*

At the end of the evening I saw a lot of guests taking home the centerpieces from the tables, which contained an assortment of gorgeous, long-stemmed white flowers. I wanted to take one home too, but had a feeling Jennifer wouldn't let that happen.

"Honey, let's go home please," I said.

"Alright, wait here, I'll get our coats and then we'll go."

Marv approached me and said, "I don't know what has come over her," in defense of his wife's behavior. "Would you like to take a centerpiece home too?" he asked in an apologetic tone.

"Yes, I would love to. Thank you so much."

Without a moment of hesitation, he picked one up and offered to carry it out to my car.

"I'm so glad you were here for Jennifer," Marv said as we walked to the parking lot.

"Thank you and I'm happy for the both of you." I felt a little awkward but wished him well as he placed the flowers on the back seat of my car. We walked back into the building. This was our first encounter in almost ten years and the ice between us had been broken. This gave me an incredible sense of peace.

Ari walked up to me with our coats and he helped me on with mine. Our ride home was quiet. Even though the ice between Marv and me had melted away, something weird had happened to the relationship with my best friend. Ari knew that I was deeply hurt and gently squeezed my hand all the way home. However, as soon as we walked through the front door, I collapsed on the sofa and burst into tears. Ari sat down next to me and held me close, while Prince was licking my salty tears. I said, "I swear Honey, I will never talk to her again." After having a good cry, I quietly crawled into bed where my wonderful husband was sleeping peacefully. I nestled close, until I drifted off to dreamland too.

First thing the next morning the telephone rang and I thanked G-d for caller ID. After several tries, I finally answered. When I heard Jennifer's voice, I immediately hung up the phone. She called back and I continued to slam the phone down, until I finally answered and said, "Okay, I'll listen."

"Dori, I was so overwhelmed by all the excitement and the guests." She continued to babble on with more excuses than I could handle.

"You didn't deserve to be treated that way and I am so very sorry."

"You really hurt me. I don't know if I can ever forgive you," I said, finally getting a word in, and then I slammed down the phone once again. She continued to call back until I forgave her. However, I wasn't certain the incident didn't damage our friendship beyond repair.

Ari and I celebrated the New Year 2000, labeled as the millennium. We had a succulent dinner and listened to the music of our favorite house guest, Frank Sinatra. We thought it best to be safe at home because of numerous rumors of possible technical malfunctions throughout the world. Diligently I stashed away tons of batteries, gallons of water and nonperishable items, just in case our world went into total darkness. Ari began singing along with Frank, "That's Life" and extended his hand to me as we danced. He twirled me around, held me close with his hand placed firmly on my lower back. We ended the night by dancing naked in our bedroom, where we brought in the new year making intense and passionate love.

This was the year we would be preparing for Zachary's Bar Mitzvah. This Jewish celebration marks the year that a boy turns 13 and is considered a man. Zachary's mom, Sheila, called and suggested we begin to work out the details of this blessed event. She had already scheduled the synagogue for May. We were also waiting to have our big closing from the sale of the store, which would happen during the summer.

Sheila and I usually got along pretty well. Often, when either one of us would go out of town we would pet sit for each other's animals. She was always nice and friendly except when she would get in a mood, when she was angry with Ari and naturally, that included me.

Sheila and her second husband, Gary, planned the entire Bar Mitzvah party. She asked me to be involved even though she had everything under control, which was fine with me. She did make arrangements for her, Gary, Ari, Zachary, Renee and me to meet for a food-tasting adventure. We wanted to hand pick the items for the menu and we were able to taste an exquisite selection of entrees. We all agreed on the menu.

Sheila did a great job planning and preparing for the party, and Ari and I agreed with everything she chose. During this time we all shared in driving Zachary to and from his Hebrew lessons. Although he hated them, he knew they were mandatory.

In our spare time, which was usually on Sundays, Ari and I would go house hunting. Considering we were never under any pressure to move, and I was our real estate broker, it made the search much more convenient.

We would look at new homes as well as commercial properties. Since we were going to come in to quite a bit of money, Ari was always on the lookout for another location. With the profits from the sale, we purchased two new commercial buildings and a small brick ranch as a rental property located right in the heart of the city. Ari and I were not only husband and wife now; we had become actual business partners and landlords, too.

Ari and I continued to complement each other with our combined knowledge and strengths, our thought process was the same too. We really enjoyed one another, both in the bedroom and in the board-room.

We loved to gamble, and we decided to welcome in the new millennium at a gambling resort on an Indian reservation in Northern Michigan. We found a hotel that had a heart shaped Jacuzzi in the room, perfect for our lifestyle. We gambled until 3:00am and then returned to our hotel room for hours of ecstasy. While Ari turned on the jets and bath water, I poured the French Vanilla bubble bath and the bubbles were gigantic, fluffy, and overflowing. We used the entire room making love until we could no longer keep our eyes open.

"I love you, Baby." he said in a faint whispery voice, as we drifted off to sleep.

Ari and I went out for dinner a couple nights before Zachary's Bar Mitzvah to have a quiet celebration honoring our third wedding anniversary. We talked about all that had happened and what we had accomplished together since we met.

"Excuse me, would you care for dessert?" the waitress asked.

"No I don't think so, I'm having my wife for dessert and she has a lot less calories."

After dinner, Ari and I went home and I quickly changed into my traditional peach lingerie.

"Catch me, catch me!" I playfully sang to him as he watched my every move.

Moments later I was caught and he embraced me by wrapping his big strong arms around me. As he laid me on the bed, while caressing my hungry body, he looked deep into my eyes and ever so slowly entered me. My entire body began to quiver and for a moment I thought I was falling off a cliff. At the same time we both screamed in ecstasy. Afterwards, we held each other and watched our wedding video for the third time, noticing how much Zachary had grown in three short years.

"There's a party goin' on right here
A celebration to last, throughout the years."

The Bar Mitzvah had arrived. Zachary was unbelievable; he read from the Torah perfectly. His intelligence and photographic memory took over and fooled all of us. He demonstrated much innocence, charm, and he was quite gorgeous too. He looked more like his father everyday and was very observant of others in his life. We would have our long special talks, and he always took me by surprise with all that he knew.

As Zachary led the service, we were all standing behind him on the *Bema* (sacred alter). Sheila and I held hands; both of us were proud of the young man that we had shared as a son. The evening proved that divided families could come together for the sake of their children, which made this special occasion even more spectacular for all of us. There were about two hundred and fifty guests and my mom came in from Florida for the special occasion, which meant a lot to me. Unfortunately, Harry and my sister could not attend. Also Mickey and Lynn, our Cancun friends, joined us for the celebration.

As the party began, I saw Zachary standing in a corner crying. His mom and other family members surrounded him. Sheila was talking to him, but obviously was not getting through, as he cried.

"Let me try," I whispered to Sheila.

"Let's go for a walk, Zach."

"What's wrong, Honey?" I tenderly asked him.

"I'm mad at Gary, he has ruined my day!" Zachary said and wiped his eyes with his jacket sleeve.

Gary is his step-dad, and they had just had a falling out. I didn't deem it necessary to ask why because the important part was for him to stop crying and feel better. I wanted him to get back to his party where his friends and family were waiting for him. And most importantly, to enjoy his big day that he so well deserved.

"Zachary, this is your special day, no one can ruin it but you. Don't let him bother you. I'm so very proud of you and everyone loves you so much. This is your day and you are the star." As I encouraged him, he nodded in agreement.

"Now let's go back to your party, and celebrate." I squeezed him tight, noticing he had stopped crying.

Everyone was seated in the ballroom, when the Disc Jockey announced the entrance of our main star. Zachary came dashing into the room with a huge smile, bouncing a basketball and everyone applauded, while rising to their feet in his honor. As is tradition, Zachary began with his candle lighting ceremony. There were fourteen candles representing the special people in his life, with an extra candle for good luck. Zachary had written something special for every person that he called up to light a candle with him.

When he called Ari and me up with him to light our candle, he referred to us as his parents, and he wrote the most beautiful words I had ever heard. While we were standing next to him lighting our candle together, I was so deeply touched that I realized a tear or two had forced their way out.

Sheila had asked me to bring my CD from the movie *Funny Girl*. Toward the end of the evening the DJ played "Don't Rain on my Parade." We all sang along with it and, at one point, he gave me the microphone thinking I could sing. I belted the song out loud not caring who heard me.

About a month later, Holly, Ari's oldest daughter called and wanted to have dinner with us; she was bringing her boyfriend Stan. This didn't happen very often; however, we were always happy to see her. At dinner she announced that she and Stan were engaged and planned to marry the following summer.

We were so thrilled for her. We hugged and kissed and congratulated them both. Although we didn't know Stan very well, he seemed like a nice, quiet young man. More importantly, he showed a great deal of love and care for Holly.

"Make whatever plans that you want, Honey. I will take care of everything," Ari volunteered happily, feeling proud that he could freely and unconditionally offer his generosity to his oldest daughter.

"If there are any wedding details you need help with, I would be honored to take care of it for you," I offered.

As Ari and I lay in bed, we thought about the exciting announcement we heard at dinner.

"Honey, this is going to be another expensive year," I mentioned.

"I know, honey, when it rains it pours," he said, as we drifted happily off to sleep.

During my first cup of coffee the next morning, the phone rang. My cousin Kathy was on the other end.

"Dori, I have something to tell you about your dad," she said and paused.

"I'm listening," I said sipping my coffee.

"My mom is going crazy. She can't take your dad living with her anymore. He's been there about a year now and has the worst living habits. The house smells like tobacco and all he does is sleep until noon. Then he demands she wait on him hand and foot. His health is deteriorating rapidly because he's not taking his meds for his disease *myasthenia gravis*. She's going crazy and it's creating real problems between my mom and her husband."

"Kathy, I'm not surprised. I haven't seen or talked with him since my wedding. Your mom, his sister, is experiencing what the rest of us have known all along."

Kathy called again ten days later.

"Dori, you won't believe this, your dad got in his old truck to drive back to Florida by himself," Kathy said.

"Thanks for letting me know Kathy. I'll talk to you later," and I hung up the phone. *Why didn't he call me to say goodbye? Why doesn't he care about me?*

Even after the wedding, when Ari and I went through all the beautiful cards, we never found one from my dad, just wishing us well. My hopes for reuniting with my dad were dashed to the ground again. As I felt a single teardrop, I knew then I would never see him again. I sincerely hoped he would make it home safely and I mentally said goodbye to him. I thought of the movie "*Yentl*" when Barbara Streisand said good-bye to her father, only her father was dead, whereas mine never actually lived. I shed a few tears as I finished my coffee realizing my life was with Ari in the present and not with an absent deadbeat father from the past.

Another eventful year had passed. We decided to celebrate my birthday and New Year's Eve on a seven night Caribbean cruise and then fly to Cancun for a seven night stay in our luxurious condo. It took three years of persuading him, but Ari finally agreed to go on a cruise. He had been wary of traveling by ship, since he had a bad experience as a child when he arrived in America. He was also hesitant because he thought he would feel confined and bored. But my husband trusted me enough to say he would give it a try.

In early January we flew to Ft. Lauderdale in the morning and boarded the ship in time for a 4:00pm sailing. As we entered the ship, the photographer snapped our picture, and he was amazed when he saw the interior of this magnificent vessel.

"Baby, this ship is a floating city. I feel like I'm in another world," he said in amazement.

As the ship began to sail, my husband loved the excellent service from the staff. We were wined, dined, and taken care of like a king and queen.

"It doesn't get much better than this," I said as I watched his reactions to all the amenities the ship offered.

Every night after dinner we enjoyed a Vegas style show with the other passengers. Then off we'd go to the casino to play a little blackjack and craps. He ended up to be a big winner almost every night and I finally broke even by the end of the week.

After being at sea for a couple of days, our first stop was the island of Jamaica. It was depressing and we felt very sad for how the natives lived. They were so poor; it was difficult to witness. As we walked through the tourist area, we found jewelry store after jewelry store.

Ari loved to go shopping on vacation because at home he never had time. As we looked in each of the shops I would seek out diamond earrings, and he would head straight for the watches. We kept calling out to one another so we could show each other our findings. We didn't buy anything in Jamaica, because he wanted to do some comparison shopping in Grand Cayman. We boarded our ship as it departed at the end of the day.

After another fantastic evening of lavish dining with our new-found friends, Ari had another winning night at the casino and I began calling him Nicky Arnstein, Fanny Brice's husband in the movie *Funny Girl*. Ari got a kick out of that and kept on winning.

"Honey, I want to renew our wedding vows for our tenth wedding anniversary," he said as he held me close.

"We can take a cruise and get remarried by the captain of the ship," I suggested.

"What a fantastic idea, I love you so much," he said.

Two days later we arrived in the Cayman Islands. One of the crew members had highly recommended a jewelry store so we went there first. As we entered this magnificent store sparkling like the evening stars, we went directly to the areas we each liked best. After a few minutes of browsing, Ari came to find me and said, "Come with me, Honey, I want to show you something. This is my bride; please show her what I picked out."

The salesman gently draped a ladies 24K rose gold watch on my wrist. The face was mother of pearl surrounded entirely by diamonds.

"This is the most gorgeous watch I have ever laid my eyes on. Please tell me more."

"The time piece is a Patek Philippe. It will increase in value, and makes a great family heirloom. Take a few minutes and see how it feels," The salesman said.

It was not only unique and the most exquisite watch I had ever seen, it was comfortable too. Meanwhile, my husband proceeded to show me what was placed on his wrist; another magnificent watch for him. The men's watch consisted of two precious stones, a ruby and a sapphire used as an intricate part of the movement and the mechanics of this fine timepiece. They were the most expensive watches in the store, probably in the world. He couldn't leave the island without these stunning his and her watches.

"Sir, would you give us a minute please?" I asked the salesperson.

"Of course, take as much time as you need," he said.

"Honey, I feel so nervous; we don't need such expensive watches." I told him.

"It's not a matter of need." *Where have I heard that line before?* "They are like buying a piece of real estate and they will increase in value, just like the salesperson said. Listen to your husband and leave the worrying to me." *I could relate to real estate and didn't say another word.*

We were drunk with excitement and began to sing the theme song from *The Jeffersons*, "Movin' On Up." We sang, and *kibbitzed* (joked around) calling each other "Wheezie" and "George". We laughed and sang, while swinging our arms together all the way back to the ship.

"Honey, I forgot to show you the earrings I found."

"Don't worry my darling, you will have those too," he assured me. *Somebody, anybody, please pinch me.*

We were back on the ship and had two days left of sailing the Caribbean Sea back to Ft Lauderdale. Our last stop was the ship's very own out island. The crew had organized an on-going BBQ, with music and the help of lots of sunshine, it was a glorious day. As our vacation came to an end we said our goodbyes to our new friends and headed for Cancun, Mexico.

"Honey, I can't wait until our next cruise. It was the best vacation I have ever had! Thank you," he said as we settled into our seats on Aeromexico.

I think the main component that has made our marriage a success is we both treat each other as the most important person in the world and everything else comes second, which is a first for me.

We arrived at our condo in Cancun and of course I wanted to get organized and unpack, while Ari relaxed at the poolside Palapa Bar. After thirty minutes of boring unpacking, I walked out on the balcony to look for my husband. *Wow, there he is, he looks so good, he should do a Banana Boat commercial.* When our eyes met, I threw him a kiss, and he raised his arm holding his favorite drink, a Chocolate Monkey.

After a light dinner and a good night's rest, we had our typical day in the resort. It began as it always did, a buffet breakfast, then we would find our chairs by the pool and lie in the sun for a couple hours until we were ready to transfer our warm tan bodies to the beach for more sun and fun. We would ride the waves in the ocean, and I could feel the sensation of the salt-water moving through my sexually aroused body.

After spending time on the beach, we went back by the pool and ordered lunch, using our lounge chairs as tables. Then we'd go back to our condo and take a soapy shower together. Rushing to my dresser drawer, I grabbed one of my sexy negligees and we made love until we were both pleased and famished.

"Who loves you?" he whispered.

"My husband loves me!" I yelled and turned towards him for another passionate kiss.

"Get dressed; I am taking you out for dinner," he said rather demandingly, which I didn't mind a bit.

On an overcast, rainy morning Ari suggested, "Honey let's go shopping, we have souvenirs to buy and it's a good day to be indoors."

So after breakfast we went to the mall for some great *shoptzing*. As we walked in and out of all the stores buying gifts for Jennifer, the kids and other family members, Ari and I noticed at the same time another beautiful jewelry store that pulled us in like a magnet.

"Look, Husband, I said, pointing to the earrings shining in the case. They are similar to the pair I didn't have a chance to show you in Grand Cayman. Do you like them?" I asked him as I held them against my ears.

"Do you want them, Honey?" he offered.

"Yes!" I said gleefully and hugged him. I realized this was why he didn't want to have any more children; because if we did, we would be home buying diapers instead.

Two weeks was a very long time to be away. A wonderful girl named Kayla from my veterinarian's office came to pet sit with Prince and Samantha in our home while we were away on vacation. I called her Nanny Kayla because she seemed to be the only person who loved Prince as much as I did. She spent a lot of time with him and even took him with her to work on Mondays. At night she would come home and watch movies with Prince by her side.

As a courtesy to me, she kept a journal of their time together, so I would have the best and funniest reading material to enjoy when I returned home. The best thing was I never had to worry about my furry children while traveling, which also gave me peace of mind.

Even though it was still very much winter in Michigan, it was good to be home and it was time to focus on Holly and her upcoming wedding in July. I called her to see if she needed any help.

"Yes, Dori, would you mind keeping track of the guest response cards from the RSVP's?" She asked.

"I would be honored," I said, happy to be involved in her wedding plans. I also received an invitation to her bridal shower given by her aunts and I wouldn't have missed it for the world.

"Dori, I hope you don't mind that I invited Sheila to the shower too. She was a very good step-mom to me when I was younger and I don't want to leave her out," Holly added.

"No problem, Honey. Sheila and I get along just fine; we'll probably end up sitting together." I said. *Oh my G-d Ari's ex-wives and I will be together for the first time.*

CHAPTER SIXTEEN

"Love and Marriage"

Frank Sinatra

It was Saturday morning, the day of Holly's bridal shower. I was looking forward to meeting everyone and a bit anxious too, but my nervous tension disappeared when I was warmly greeted by Holly's aunts and grandmother. Sheila was already there, and we hugged each other hello.

"Dori, I saved a seat next to me, if you want," she said, pointing to the table.

"Thank you, that's great."

Unfortunately, Holly's mom wasn't feeling well, so meeting her would just have to wait until the wedding. After lunch, Holly's Aunt Olivia (Ari's ex sister in-law) and I happened to be in the ladies room at the same time. We ended up enjoying small talk and having a cigarette together. She was such a doll.

I went to check on Holly to see how she was holding up.

"How are you doing, honey?"

"I'm fine now but I'm really nervous about the wedding. My mom and dad's families haven't been in the same room together in years, let along spoken to one another.

"Don't worry, they're all adults and everything will be fine. You're the important one and your love and marriage are all that matters."

"Thank you, Dori,"

We shared a hug and off she went to mingle with her guests. The shower was wonderful, and she received many beautiful gifts.

When I got home later, I explained to Ari how nervous Holly was about both families being together at the wedding. He shared with me that there had been a great deal of animosity between him and his ex-in-laws, during and after the divorce. Since I was not in his life back then, I considered myself on neutral ground and would be there for Holly unconditionally.

On July 14, 2001, we arrived at the hall for Ari's daughter's wedding.

When my husband and I walked in, we immediately saw Holly, her mother Janie, and her grandparents, standing by her side. Holly nervously made the introductions. To my surprise, Janie and I had a warm connection right away. It seemed that any bitterness that existed between these families many years ago had dissipated into thin air. I then took a moment to check on Holly.

"How are you doing, honey?" I asked gently, taking her hand.

217

"I just took some Pepto Bismol because my stomach is killing me," she confided.

"You look absolutely breathtaking and as you can see, everything is just fine. Isn't your man waiting to marry you? Now go and be happy."

"Love and marriage, love and marriage
Go together like a horse and carriage."

The ceremony was beautiful and since Ari was giving his daughter away, he and I couldn't walk down the aisle together, so Zachary was my escort. After I was seated, I watched him take his place with the other groomsmen. He stood so tall and proud, which made me realize how much he had matured since his Bar Mitzvah only a year earlier. As I watched my husband *kvell* (beam with pride) as he gave his daughter away, I could tell he was elated over her extraordinary beauty and happiness.

After dinner, the music was playing and I had a fun idea. Since I love to do things spontaneously, I went up to Sheila and asked her to dance. Without hesitation, she accepted and we walked straight to the dance floor. While we were dancing, she said,

"Let's go get wife number one."

The two of us found Janie and pulled her on to the dance floor and the three of us danced in a circle. Then suddenly, to everyone's astonishment, my husband entered the circle and the three of us danced around him. By this time the guests were roaring, and he was in his glory. I hoped Holly was getting a glimpse of all this. We all had a fantastic time and the peace process had taken place.

"The day that changed America."

Early one Tuesday morning I was having coffee and I turned on the television to check the latest news and weather. I wasn't paying attention until I heard the explosion and screams coming from the television. There had been some kind of explosion in New York. I stopped cold, sat down and watched in horror. The words 'Breaking Story' flashed on the screen. A plane had crashed into the World Trade Center. Oh my G-d, a second plane had hit another tower. It was September 11, 2001, the day America changed forever. I panicked and began to cry, while dialing my husband's cell phone.

"I know honey. I have already heard the news, it's everywhere," he said, his voice tense.

"I'm not getting on a plane for a very long time," I told him.

"Honey, you can't allow these terrorists to stop you from living," he said and added, "Ok baby, I have to go now, I'll try to be home early. I love you."

"Amazing grace, how sweet the sound."

Thirty days after that horrific day in New York, my mom called with more bad news. The sights and sounds from 9/11 were permanently stamped in our minds.

"Hello, Dori, is that you?" Her voice was shaking.

"Hi, Mom, yes it's me, what's wrong?"

"I have some very bad news."

There was total silence.

"What, mom, what is it?" I asked in desperation.

"Harry died," she announced and I suddenly felt sick inside.

In a sense, we had lost Harry a long time ago, when he had had his stroke. I couldn't believe he was actually gone, and I would never see him again.

As the tears drenched my face, I realized now why he had been detaching himself from my sister and me.

"Mom, please don't be mad at me. Because of the tragedy at the World Trade Center, I am too petrified to fly. I can't come in and be with you."

"I'll be fine. Harry has a lot of friends here and they have been a great source of comfort and support. Is Lori afraid to fly, too?" She asked. Her voice was frail and shaking. *Oh my G-d I feel so bad.*

"I don't know, but I promise I'll come down and help you as soon as things calm down," I told her and wiped my eyes.

As we said our goodbyes, I told her I loved her, unsure if she had heard me.

As I sat alone, my guilt began to take over. I was trying to justify why I wasn't flying to Florida to be with Mom in her time of need. I didn't want to leave the man I had finally found after a lifetime of searching. I didn't want to take any chances.

I sat and reflected on Harry's life and how he had become like a father to Lori and me. I thought of how he always remembered our birthdays and was concerned about the men I dated. He was very protective of me, which made me feel I had someone to lean on. My step-dad was my only family member that stood by my side when I married Ari. I knew I would miss him so much for many years to come.

I gave Lori a call; Mom had already told her about Harry.

"Hi Lori, I have a question. Are you going to fly to Florida?"

"Why wouldn't I?" she asked.

"Good, cause I'm too scared to fly," I admitted.

"You are always scared," she said, and I could tell she was shaking her head back and forth.

We made arrangements to check back with each other later that day to arrange a flight for her to Florida. Later the same day, Lori called back.

"Mom doesn't want me to fly there either; she said she'll be fine."

I continued to call Mom every day before and after Harry's funeral, to see how she was and to tell her that I loved her. Each time I talked with her my guilt continued to grow. It had been a few days since the funeral and mom would call and cry, which was so hard to deal with, being so far apart. Sometimes she would be so upset I couldn't make out what she was saying.

After a few months, the phone calls became a little bit easier. As time past, her inner strength began to take over and there were more good days than bad. However, inside I had a growing anger toward her. I was mad because during the last few years of her marriage all she did was complain about her life with Harry. She hated where she lived and never had anything positive to say about their home. A new resentment toward her had set in my heart.

Harry was someone I loved very much, and now he was gone forever too. Harry's death hit me hard. I felt as if Mom had robbed me of a father my entire life. I know the men in her life were her choices but she never asked me about my pain and anger from losing dad after dad. I realize her decisions to divorce were not intentional toward me, but she wasn't compassionate about how I was affected by these painful losses which hurt me deeply. At the core of it all was that Mom had never been satisfied with anything or anyone. It seemed nothing could ever fill the hole in her soul that always tormented her. Harry seemed to bring her happiness and stability, which only satisfied her for a short while. On the other hand she had always been my best friend and I loved her, *Kvetching* (complaining) and all.

Ari and I were still looking for our dream home together. We had found a few possibilities; however, there was always something that wasn't right. Either the inspection didn't work out or the builder was trying to rip us off with the upgrades. The real estate market had been soft since 9/11. It was definitely a buyer's market, so it was a good time to buy.

One Sunday morning I decided to check the MLS (Multiple Listing Service) on the internet for any new listings. I found a few and set up appointments for us to see them that afternoon.

The first house we walked into was a three bedroom brick ranch located in a beautiful subdivision. It was situated on a cul-de-sac, surrounded by dozens of trees. It is actually a freestanding site condo, which means everyone has their own lot, but the outside maintenance is taken care of by the association.

"Wow, Ari, the way the sub is set up, everyone has woods behind them." I was impressed and getting excited.

"Relax honey, let's wait and see," he suggested. The house was about two thousand square feet with a contemporary flair, with soaring high ceilings and angled walls adding to the beauty. The minute I walked in, I knew it was perfect for us, although I did keep quiet for a change. A single elderly man lived there and the décor throughout was dark and gloomy with dark brown window treatments and dark brown carpeting.

My experience selling new construction allowed me to see beyond the unsightly décor and the beauty it was covering up. The listing agent, Terry Wolf, was showing us through and when we went down the basement, there was more space than we could ever have imagined. We also had privacy and beautifully landscaped grounds, where I could plant my flowers. I nodded my head toward Ari and gave him the look. He nodded back to me, giving me the go ahead.

"Terry, we want to make an offer."

We negotiated for less than a minute and the deal was made. I was able to apply my selling commission to the sales price, which reduced it greatly. Ari and I were both ecstatic as we went through all the motions of buying this home over the next few weeks. Our mortgage approval went smoothly, and we were able to close in December of 2001.

Later that day after the closing, when Ari was on his way home from work, I called him and invited him to drive to the new house instead.

"No problem, honey, I will see you soon," he said. When he walked into our new house he shook his head and smiled.

I had placed an unopened bottle of champagne with plastic champagne glasses on the floor. I had dinner delivered and we ate it in front of the blazing fireplace. After Ari popped the cork on the bottle of bubbly, we toasted each other with intertwined arms.

"Love makes a house a home."

For the next few months I was very busy. I had listed my condo for sale while simultaneously looking for a construction company for some major renovation before we moved in. Eventually, I found just the right company owned by two brothers and they made the changes I wanted trouble-free. I had them renovate everything from the flooring, to the electrical, to repainting the entire house.

We had a finish carpenter build dramatic floor to ceiling pillars in front of the fireplace along with a three-tiered mantle, painted in white semi-gloss. The new color scheme would be dark taupe walls with white trim throughout the house. After deciding to change the handles on the white kitchen cabinets from white plastic to a soft silver metal, this eventually became my accent color throughout our home.

My husband gave me free reign to change the look of the house. His only requests were a dry sauna installed in the basement, a wet sauna in the master bedroom, and a big screen television in the living room. We eventually wanted to finish the lower level with state of the art exercise equipment and a pool table to reactivate his long untouched talents.

While the renovation was going on, Ari and I took our annual one week vacation at our resort in Cancun over New Year's. After our return, the new house was ready for us to move in. We received an offer on the old condo and after making a few minor changes on the purchase agreement, we were able to close.

Having made many calls and conducting many interviews, I realized I couldn't find a decorator I liked because they wouldn't give me any personal freedom nor could I make a move without them. So I decided to decorate and furnish myself. *I've always depended on me, so why stop now?* After 6 months of measuring and *shoptzing,* my decorating extravaganza was finished. The entire look of the home had become beautiful, open, light, airy, romantic, sexy, and functional to boot. When Ari would come home from work, all he would say is "Wow!" We agreed we were never moving.

Zachary, whom we saw once a week if not more, was growing like a weed. We had a very close special relationship with each other. Renee was busy with her dancing career and Holly was busy with her new husband. We didn't see his daughters as much as we would have liked, but they kept in touch by calling. Since her wedding, Holly and I were building a great friendship through e-mails and meeting for our special lady lunches, which meant so much to me. We had very little contact with Ari's eldest son Evan, who seemed to be busy working and kept to himself.

CHAPTER SEVENTEEN

"Bad Case of Loving You (Doctor, Doctor)"

Robert Palmer

"I want to get gastric bypass surgery," Jennifer told me one day out of the clear blue.

She had always been a little *zaftig* (a bit on the heavy side), and now she was toying with the idea of gastric bypass surgery to help her in her weight loss efforts. She was turning 50 the following year and this made her consider making a drastic change. She also wanted a huge birthday celebration and hinted she wanted me to plan it.

"This is for your husband, Marv, to plan, not me," I told her, and I had a feeling I would be involved more than I wanted.

Ari seemed to be extra tired lately and I felt he needed a few days off to rest and relax, but I knew he wouldn't do it on his own. So I mailed him a special invitation for a three-day rendezvous with me and requested him to R.S.V.P. via my cell phone. A couple of days later, Ari called and graciously accepted.

The following Saturday, his long weekend of rest and relaxation would begin. After sleeping in and having breakfast, we went out looking at cars and then to an art gallery. He didn't get much rest because after a nice easy day, we headed for the casino and went to work gambling the night away. Sunday, we both needed to sleep late. I brought him a cup of coffee and the paper while he rested in bed. He was feeling frisky and ended up chasing me around the house. He caught me and we made love on the white sheep skin rug in front of the fireplace before breakfast.

As his mini-vacation continued on Monday, I made an appointment at a local health spa using our gift card that we had received at Chanukah from my in-laws. I reserved a 'couple's delight,' which included his and her massages, followed by a private Jacuzzi bath, where we were served champagne and fresh fruit. His time away from the stores came to an end, but it had been wonderful spending precious time with my husband.

"Papa, can you hear me?"

It was a beautiful fall evening in October 2002, and we had just come home from dinner.

"Honey, there goes the phone, can you get it. I'm jumping in the shower?" he said.

"Hello," I said answering the phone.

"Is this Dori Weitzman?"

"No. I mean yes, that was my maiden name." I said slightly embarrassed.

"Is your father Jacob Weitzman?"

"Yes," I said slowly sitting down at the kitchen table.

"I'm a friend and neighbor of your dad's from Florida. He was just taken by ambulance to the hospital. I think he's dead." His voice cracked a little.

"Can you hold on a moment please?" I asked him.

I wanted to conference call my Aunt Darlene, who is my dad's sister. With my sweaty palm slipping on the phone in one hand, I dialed her number watching my forefinger shake with the others.

"Aunt Darlene, I have this friend of dad's on the line and he is saying dad had been taken to the hospital and he thinks he's dead. Will you talk to him with me on a conference call?"

"Of course, honey," she said and the three of us were on the line.

I was totally silent while my aunt responded to all the details. She agreed to handle everything. The man confirmed his death and hung up as we discussed what needed to be done. She agreed to handle all the arrangements. She was extremely understanding and compassionate about how I felt. She was aware that my tears and feelings for him had been frozen in time long ago. She planned on holding a memorial service for him in her home because he wished to be cremated.

After we finished talking I ran to tell Ari the news where he was drying off from his steam shower. With his warm and moist body, he held me close and squeezed me tight. Then I immediately called my mom and sister.

"Dori, darling, he just did the best he could do, even though he wasn't any part of our lives," Mom said.

Even though she complained a lot about her life, she always had a kind word for everyone.

"Papa can you see me?"

As I hung up the phone I could feel the waves of pain washing throughout my body. Knowing this is final and the piece of my daddy pie will forever be missing. *Will I ever have closure?*

A few days later, my dad was cremated and his remains were placed on a shelf at the mortuary until his brother Terry could go down to Florida to pick them up. The memorial service was held in my aunt's home here in Detroit the same day my dad was cremated in Florida. Holly and Zachary were there along with my in-laws, family, and friends. It was comforting to see that these people were here for me. However, the rabbi refused to do the service, because the Jewish religion does not recognize cremation. So, Aunt Darlene asked Ari to lead the service, which he did with tenderness and love.

About six months later I was talking to my cousin Kathy on the telephone.

"Kathy, did Uncle Terry (my dad's brother) ever get down to Florida to pick up my dad's remains?" I asked.

"No Dori, not that I know of," she answered.

"Isn't this crazy?" I asked shaking my head and thinking back to that young spoiled man who was born with a silver spoon in his mouth and now ended up in a silver urn.

"He was nowhere in life and now he's nowhere in death," she said. This was the most profound statement I had ever heard.

After the New Year's holiday, Ari and I decided it was time to start looking for a new car for me. We were planning to give my triple black Toyota Celica convertible to Zachary when he turned sixteen, which wouldn't be until next March.

We gave Zachary the option of getting a new car of his choice within a certain price range or my old car. Even though it was eight years old, it was in great condition inside and out. Ari gave him one condition; he had to get a part-time job and show some responsibility before he would be given a car. Zachary agreed and began working part time at the deli. He decided he wanted my car, so Ari and I had to start looking for a new car for me.

Thanksgiving had come quickly that year, and it was my turn to host this festive holiday in our new home. There are thirteen family members in Ari's immediate family, including us. The menu was planned in advance, and I went to the market a couple of days before. My mother gave me her famous turkey recipe I have held on to for years, hoping one day I would give it a try. I also made a kosher turkey breast especially for my sister-in-law, a sweet potato soufflé, and a noodle *kugel* that screams high cholesterol. Everyone flipped over it. I served a huge field green salad with vegetables and a touch of dried cherries. I also served asparagus, whipped garlic mashed potatoes, and an old family favorite, *kishka*.

It was such a big hit that my new family voted me to host next Thanksgiving, too. The only thing that was missing was Mom and Lori, but I knew they would have been proud of me. Since keeping my promise to

Ari, cooking in the kitchen has been a rarity and cooking in the bedroom is more the norm and a lot more exciting. *Honor thy husband, that's what they say.*

Since entertaining our family for the Thanksgiving holiday was such a great success, we decided to have a New Year's party for a few good friends. Ari loved the idea because we would be home and not out driving around with all the crazy drunk drivers. We had about ten of our closest friends for an elegant sit down dinner with music and dancing.

At midnight Ari and I cuddled together on the sofa with our friends gathered around us. We all lifted our glasses in a toast to say good-bye to 2002 and hello to 2003 while watching the ball drop with Dick Clark on TV.

Ari and I went to the Detroit Auto show the first week in January to see what was new for this year. Over the winter months we kept our eyes open for the right car and test drove many of them. Finally, we found and bought our dream car.

It was a hot, fast, black and sexy convertible. Lexus designed the SC 430 just for us. It had a cream leather interior and a dashboard trimmed in maple, a perfect match to our taste. The car did everything but fly. I must admit, I was a bit intimidated, and it took me a good month to be comfortable driving it.

Zachary was very excited about turning sixteen in March. Of course we were nervous wrecks because he was growing up so fast, and soon he would be driving my little black sports car that was waiting for him.

During this time Zachary had been getting into fights with his mother, which for the most part was a normal thing for a teenager.

"Dad, please can I move in with you guys? I can't take it any more!" Zachary begged his dad in a state of panic.

We welcomed him into our home. Of course, it was quite an adjustment for Ari and me. *Goodbye sexy lingerie and hello flannel pajamas.* But we felt we made the right decision. Ari and I planned on building a room downstairs, so Zachary would have his privacy. I called our construction man and we came up with a suitable floor plan. I was ready to get to work; however, Ari being the cautious man that he is, wanted us to wait until he filed for joint physical custody of Zachary.

Two and a half months later, Zachary's mother Sheila began calling Zachary and pleading with him to return home to live with her. Though he was torn, he wanted the same thing. After talking with Ari, Zachary decided to go back to his mother's home.

We were crushed by his decision, but we respected it. We didn't want Zachary to suffer any more than he already had, so his dad drove him back home to his mother's house, no questions asked. After Ari returned, he walked into the house with his head hanging low. Then he fell into my arms and cried like a baby. I held him close as tears ran down my cheeks as well.

We talked about it and promised each other never to go through that again. After three short months, Zachary was gone and the house was filled with a different kind of silence. We didn't hear from him, which I sort of understood because he needed time to sort things out.

Samantha, my eighteen-year-old cat was very sick, and I took her to the vet. After a brief exam, the vet and I agreed that it was time to put her down.

She was the first thing in my life with some sort of permanence, but I couldn't let her suffer anymore. I sat in the lobby and cried while the vet and Nanny Kayla put her to sleep forever.

A few weeks later, I received a sympathy card from my vet. It was such a beautiful card and made me feel as if I had been a good mommy to her and that I had done the right thing. I cried as I read the card, but it also brought me great comfort.

Jennifer went for an evaluation with the gastric bypass surgeon, and he qualified her for the surgery. As serious as the operation was, Jennifer acted as if it was no big *metsiyeh* (deal). She wanted to look and feel great for her fiftieth birthday party. I was petrified and I didn't like the idea of her having major surgery to lose weight. My concern for her grew in equal proportion to her excitement to be thin. I would be there for her, no matter how scared I was. Her surgery was scheduled for June.

During this time, Ari's business partner and best friend of thirty years was burned out and wanted to retire. After talking back and forth, they parted on a negative note, and Ari never heard from him again. This loss was devastating to him and it created a void in his life. He mourned his loss of friendship but continued to move forward in his business and personal life.

About a month later, Zachary finally called us to have dinner. When we picked him up, it was obvious he didn't want to talk about his abrupt move-out, which was acceptable to his dad. And though I didn't approve of it, I went along with my husband's decision.

Zachary's sixteenth birthday had finally arrived. His dad took him to get his driver's license, and Zach passed the written test and the road test with flying colors. Now it was time to let my favorite car go. By now I had gotten use to driving my new car and I even had a vanity plate made for it, which read, LVEHIM.

As I handed the keys to Zachary, I was hesitant and a bit uncomfortable. I realized that the car would still be in the family, but Zachary was only sixteen and I was concerned for his safety. He happily took the keys, kissed us, and off he went.

About a week later, the ringing of the telephone woke Ari from his nap and he finally grabbed it on the third ring.

"Hello. Yes, this is he," he said, while sitting straight up in bed.

"What? No! Yes, yes I'll be right there." Ari hung up the phone and I looked at him, the color drained from his face.

"What is it?" I asked worriedly.

"They're holding Zachary at the police station, we have to go now!"

"Is he hurt?" I asked frantically.

"The cop wouldn't tell me anything!"

I grabbed my purse and keys as we flew out the door. We were silently frightened not knowing what to expect when we arrived at the police station. *What if he's behind bars?*

As soon as we walked into the front lobby of the police station, we saw him sitting all by himself on a chair, looking at the ground. It turned out he received two speeding tickets within thirty minutes of each other in two different cities.

"Dad, I was so lost, I called my sister for directions and I wasn't paying attention. I didn't realize how fast I was going," he said hysterically through tear-filled eyes. Since I had no sense of direction myself, I understood his dilemma completely. I drove my old car home and we decided not to let him have the car for a very long time.

A few months later Zachary had his day in court. His mother took him, along with a family friend who was an attorney. There were two court dates with two different judges and both of them went very easy on him. Zachary got off with a small fine and one year of probation.

He was very depressed because he lost his freedom and independence. Even though he understood why the car was taken away, it was still very difficult for him to live with. However, he did have access to a car at home with his mother, and I would drive him anywhere he needed to go when he would ask. Zachary is a terrific kid and how he handled this experience without anger or resentment is stupendous. Although this was a difficult first lesson for him to learn, he was handling it like a man. Zachary is very special and my heart went out to him; however, I knew this experience would enhance his growth and he would continue to mature into a beautiful young man.

It was a typical Monday morning for everyone else except for Jennifer. She was on her way to the hospital for major surgery. When I arrived at the hospital, I went straight to the waiting room, where Marv and her friend Pauline were already seated. He was a nervous wreck and in tears. It was the worst waiting room anxiety I had ever known.

"Doctor, doctor, give me the news."

"What's going on? Have you heard anything, yet?"
"No," Marv answered hastily.
We all sat patiently waiting for the surgeon to come out and tell us about the surgery. The unknown

was the worst part. Pauline and I went to grab a snack from the cafeteria, and then, about twenty minutes after returning, the surgeon came into the waiting room. Pauline and I grabbed each other's hands and squeezed.

"The surgery went well; she is in recovery right now. In about thirty minutes they'll take her to her room, where you can see her," he told us and we thanked him. We all breathed a sigh of relief.

We made our way up to her floor and waited outside her room, while they transferred her from the gurney to her bed. I loved her so much and I was so relieved that she was awake and the surgery was over. The nurse came out and gave us the go ahead to come in and see her. As I looked at the tubes connected to her I kissed her pale face, forcing a smile.

"I'm fine, Dori, I'm fine," she said with a smile. She knew I was worried. The smells of the hospital and the sight of my best friend lying helplessly in the bed with major bandages and all hooked up to a million monitors caused me to feel heated and nauseated. Then I began to feel dizzy, and I grabbed a chair next to the bed for support.

Pauline came into the room and saw I wasn't doing well. She walked me out and the next thing I remembered was waking up in a wheelchair in the hallway outside of Jen's room.

"It's okay, honey, you just fainted," one of the nurses said as Pauline wiped the moisture from my forehead. They insisted I go to the emergency room but I refused. Pauline gave me a sip of orange juice that she had gotten from the nurse's station.

"You need the sugar, Dori," she said as I gradually sipped the refreshing juice.

"I'm fine, Pauline, really; it was probably just from seeing Jennifer all hooked up. I'll go to my doctor as soon as possible for a check-up," I assured her.
I went back in to say goodbye to my dear friend who lay helplessly in bed. Nothing can ever happen to her.

"Even now you're stealing my thunder," she joked in a weak voice.

"I'm so sorry Jennifer, I don't know what happened. I'll come and see you when you get home in a few days," I told her and kissed her again on the forehead.

Marv and Pauline walked me out to my car. I wasn't sure what had happened to me either, but I planned on getting a thorough check up.

Over the next couple of months I went to doctors galore and had every part of my body tested. I had major blood work, CAT scans, and every heart test there is. And all results came back negative. So I chalked it up to just getting upset over Jennifer's condition.

About a month later I had another episode as I was driving on the expressway at full speed to pick up mom at the airport. Terrified, I pulled over to the shoulder of the road and began to cry uncontrollably. I grabbed my cell phone and quickly dialed 911. Believe it or not, the line was busy. I dialed Ari.

"Honey, I can't drive to the airport to pick up my mom."

"What's wrong, honey? You sound awful." Ari heard the panic in my voice.

"I don't know. Something is seriously wrong with me."

"Do you have bottled water with you?" He asked.

"Yes, honey." I said as I fumbled for the bottle sitting in the cup holder.

"Good, now drink some water and I will stay with you on the phone until you get home safely." He then assured me he'd leave work right away and go pick up my mom.

As soon as I got into the house, I felt better, but I was shaken with worry. All I could do was lie on the couch and hug Prince while anxiously waiting for my husband and mother to come home.

They walked in the house within a couple of hours. I was so relieved they were home safely. This was the very first time I didn't pick my mom up at the airport since she left Michigan many years earlier. I'm sure she was shocked to see my husband instead of me. I ended up being sick the entire time mom was here and I landed back in the hospital.

It turned out my blood pressure was sky high and out of control, and I was low on magnesium. After a few hours, the doctor released me, prescribed medication, and told me to follow up with my own doctor.

I'm feeling much better now; however, as a result of all this, I stay away from hospitals and I no longer drive on expressways.

Jennifer's recovery was extremely slow. During her healing process, she was supposed to be drinking liquid protein drinks whenever she felt hungry. However, she hated the taste of them and was refusing to drink them. At this point, since she wasn't taking in any protein, her energy level dropped, and she became depressed.

As time went on, Jennifer began to regain her strength. Her doctor made an adjustment on her medication, and she finally got back to her jovial self. The weight was dropping rapidly and her looks began to change. But the greatest improvement was that she was happier and more upbeat then she had ever been.

Her personality was alive with joy along with her new zest for life. She had an excitement and appreciation for everything, including her brand new body.

"Dori, how would you feel about having my 50th birthday party at your house and Marv would pay for everything?" Jennifer asked as we were gabbing on the phone.

"Let me talk to Ari and see how he feels about it and I'll let you know," I told her.

I called Jennifer the next day. "Ari had no problem with it whatsoever. He even offered to cater your party if you want him to," I added. After giving Jen the great news, she was elated.

"Sounds great, Dori, you're the best!"

"How about if I design and mail the invitations, do the bar, and take care of the decorating?" I offered and she was thrilled. We both knew it would be a fun celebration. Together Jennifer and I set the date for Saturday, September 20, 2003.

Due to her recent surgery and her having become the newly self-elected chief of the fashion police, I wanted to add to her new wardrobe that she so desperately wanted. Her newfound love of life and her new reality of smaller sizes couldn't keep her out of the stores. I promised when she reached her goal weight I would take her on a shopping spree. I wanted her to feel like the character from the movie *Pretty Woman*.

"Dori, I won't have anything to open from you at my party, right? She said sadly, switching gears from happy to worried. *The child in her was talking, that's my Jen.*

"Don't be concerned, I will have something for you to open," I assured her and with that, Jennifer was content.

A couple of weeks later, I mailed seventy-five handmade invitations to Jennifer's closest friends. After all these years, her husband (my ex), my husband and I were now giving a party for my best friend. However, I felt comfortable and believed it was the right thing to do. My biggest concern was if our home was big enough to hold seventy-five people eating and drinking at the same time.

"Don't agonize over this, Dori; a lot of people won't come," Jennifer would constantly tell me.

Jennifer's party plans were in full swing. We ended up with about fifty-five guest responses. Marv kept thanking me every chance he had. I felt very good inside, and it reaffirmed that I definitely was doing the right thing.

"The rising floodwaters."

At about two in the morning, one week before the party, Ari frantically woke me up.

"Honey, wake up, get up now!" I tried to ignore him, but he persisted.

"What is it, Honey?" I mumbled under the covers.

"Honey, get up! Our entire house is flooded!" He said.

"What?" I said in a fog of confusion.

I shot straight up in bed and went directly to the kitchen to check on Prince where he was whimpering in his crate. *Oh my G-d, the kitchen is filling up with water.* I grabbed my dog while we watched Ari frantically searching for the shut off valve that he couldn't find. In the meantime, I dialed 911. Minutes later, the fire department arrived and found the problem immediately. A pipe had burst underneath the kitchen sink.

They covered our furniture with tarps in the lower level because the drop ceiling had collapsed. They helped us absorb the water with every towel I could find in the house. The West Bloomfield Fire Department was wonderful.

We looked at our beautiful home that, in a matter of minutes, was in shambles. Our maple wood floor was buckling and completely ruined. Ari was visibly shaken, and he held me.

"It could have been worse, Honey. At least we still have our home and we're not physically hurt," I said comforting him.

After a few hours of sleep, I got up and called the insurance company. They assured me a disaster crew would be at the house within a few hours. As promised, they arrived and began inspecting the house.

Suddenly, my house was swarming with inspectors as they checked out every square inch of the house. They immediately began the cleanup by placing gigantic and loud commercial fans throughout, which were to run non-stop for three full days. Another crew arrived to clean out the tremendous amount of debris.

"When can you start working on replacing all the damaged items?" I asked, telling him about Jennifer's party.

"We will have the house cleaned up by Friday afternoon, just in time for your party on Saturday. Then we will begin the restoration on Monday," he assured me as he continued his work. I took his word as gospel and called Jen.

"I have good news and bad news, which one do you want first?" I told Jennifer on the phone.

"I want the bad news first," she said with hesitancy.

"Okay, last night our house flooded and it's in shambles. Our maple wood floors are totally ruined. They have to be completely torn out and replaced."

"Oh Dori, are you guys okay? Oh, oh, what about the party?" she asked, realizing her big night was this weekend.

"Well, how about the good news?" I offered.

"Okay, what's the good news?" she waited.

"The good news is they will have the house cleaned up by Friday, so we can have your party as planned." I said, pacing my words to drag out her anticipation, as a *kibbitz* (just for fun).

"That's great. Wow, what a relief," she said.

In just a few short days, the house looked pretty good, almost as if nothing had happened. The only part they couldn't temporarily fix was my wood floors.

On Saturday morning, I was very busy setting up the decorations. I filled the bar, set the tables, and was having a ball placing the funny 'Over the Hill' signs and banners up in Jennifer's honor. The balloons were the final touch and Jennifer's friend Pauline was bringing them. Ari brought in the deli trays along with a fruit boat made out of a watermelon. It was all so exciting that I couldn't wait for the party to start.

Jennifer was definitely the star that night. She looked great and everyone went nuts over her new look. Since her surgery she had lost over fifty pounds. She looked like a doll, pretty in pink and making a serious fashion statement from head to toe.

Though she did get some gag gifts, she received many nice personal gifts as well. The party, with all the *tumel* (activity, noise) turned out to be an enormous success and then some.

The next week was rough for Ari and me. We moved Prince and some of our belongings to a hotel, so the repair team could have free reign of the house. They needed a full five days to complete the work. The insurance company took care of everything. In fact, they mailed the expense check for our hotel stay in advance. When the restoration was complete, along with our brand new maple floor in place, the moving company moved all of our furniture back in and it was home sweet home once again, as if we had never left.

Jennifer kept in touch during the week and she couldn't stop talking about her party. She kept repeating herself by telling me how much she loved me and her party was the best. I also received a beautiful thank you note that expressed her feelings, something Jen doesn't do very often. I remember one line in particular. *"Friends are like diamonds, forever."*

After I read the card in excess of five times thinking about the party and the flood, I was so happy it all worked out in the end. *I think I'm finally prepared to double date with my ex. I know, G-d, when we plan, you laugh.*

After years of refusing to go out with Marv and Jennifer, I finally gave in and agreed. Since Marv and I were on speaking terms, there was no harm in going out to dinner together. The plans were made for the four of us to go out for dinner to our favorite Italian restaurant, The Big P, three weeks from Saturday.

The first and last time I double dated with Jennifer was when I flew in from Dallas for a visit to meet Marv back in 1985. Since Jen and I never socialized together, this became even more exciting. Sometimes life takes some crazy turns.

She was anticipating a great time and I had no idea what to think. *I can't imagine the four of us actually sitting at a table having dinner as if this were an everyday occurrence.* Jennifer, of course, had to *shpotz* for the perfect outfit. So we spent our typical Saturday afternoon getting retail therapy.

Ari and I met Jennifer and Marv about 7:30 at the bar in The Big P. Ari bought a round of drinks and everyone was really warming up. We all stood around talking and laughing away, while waiting to be seated. Jennifer and I were *plotzing* (going nuts) while watching our husbands talking and getting along. Her mile wide smile said it all.

Seeing the glow of happiness on Jennifer's face was sheer joy. After we were seated, all of us lifted our glasses in a toast to good food and good friends, and then we burst out laughing. To our surprise the evening was over before we knew it, and we all had had a great time. We were already talking about getting together again soon.

As time went on, Jennifer and Marv became our new best friends. Our husbands got along famously, and I was impressed with the respect everyone showed each other.

Jennifer and I had never been so close and now that she had lost so much weight we began to dress alike too. When we would go to the mall, anything that I liked and bought, she liked and bought, too. On Saturday nights when the four of us were going out, we would plan our twin-like outfits and sometimes plan the guy's clothes too.

Now with her brand new body, Jennifer had scheduled her next surgical procedure, a nip and tuck, *Oy Vey*. Her healing had gone well after her gastric bypass surgery; however, she did develop a hernia. This is very common for patients. She and her doctor, whom she loved and trusted agreed, when he did the nip and tuck, he would remove what she called her little baby. Jennifer had lost over one hundred pounds by then and she looked beautiful. Her new body and great looks gave her tremendous confidence, freedom and a new lease on life. She was exuberant and dripping in happiness not only on the outside, but from the inside, too. It was fully understood that I wasn't going to be at the hospital this time. I didn't want a repeat.

Come on phone ring, I can't stand this waiting, I'm so scared. Dear G-d, please take care of my Jen.

Finally I got the call from her friend Pauline.

"Jen's surgery went well. She's bandaged up pretty severely around her arms and stomach. And she will have a long healing process. You know Jen, she'll be fine because nothing can keep her down for long."

"Thank you so much for letting me know, please give her a kiss for me."

After Marv brought her home, I immediately went to their house and was thrilled to see her up and around. We were all relieved that her nip and tuck had gone well. Now her only problem was that she couldn't stop buying those low cut jeans.

The Big Chill

To my surprise, I received an invitation from a few of my high school friends. They had planned a huge 50th birthday party weekend and called it the "Big Chill" to be held at the end of October. The place was three hours away and was open to everyone in the class, mainly because our entire class was turning fifty years old.

However, there was one major problem; spouses or significant others were not invited. This was a problem for me, since Ari was my life and my first priority. However, as much as I wanted to go, I would never leave Ari for an entire weekend, so I declined the invitation.

A few weeks later, I received news that one of my former classmates, Darla, had lost her father. I had known Darla since kindergarten. A group of us went to the funeral. Following the service, one of the girls brought up the "Big Chill' party and tried to convince me to go, and of course I declined again. A couple of days later, I received an e-mail that read: "Significant others are welcome."

After talking to Ari and telling him the good news, I responded with a yes to the e-mail. We decided to drive up on Saturday for a one-night stay.

I called Tammy, one of Prince's pet sitters, who would always take care of him when Nanny Kayla wasn't available.

"I have a horse show that same week-end and I won't be able to stay at your house, but I have a great idea. Let me take Prince with me and he'll have so much fun," she offered.

"No Tammy, he's too old," I told her. But after promising me she wouldn't let him out of her sight, I agreed.

"Okay. Why not? Prince deserves some fun in his golden years, too," I told her, realizing my precious boy would be fourteen years old, which is equal to ninety-eight in doggie years. Prince was my second longest commitment, right after Samantha. For the most part, he was doing well for his advanced age. He took his dog vitamins like a champ and was never ill. Once in awhile, Ari would bring him a little bit of corned beef, which he had grown to expect.

Unfortunately, Prince was experiencing the same common ailments of old age as humans do. He had the worst case of bad breath, his motor skills had slowed and arthritis had set in. I had to carry him in and out of the house to do his personal business because of his weak back and legs. But as long as my Prince was happy and living the good life, he would continue to bring joy to mine.

We arrived in Caseville, Michigan in about three hours. I was a bit nervous, like I was going to my high school reunion, but I relaxed when we were greeted with open arms by my old friends.

A few of the guys brought their instruments and played classic rock songs from our high school days. They began playing "You Can't Always Get What You Want," and I went straight to the microphone to sing the chorus. The rest of the girls became my back-up singers.

Later that evening, after dinner and a little rock and roll, one of our classmates brought out this gorgeous chocolate birthday cake decorated with white roses. The cake read Happy 50th; only this time the number 50 was meant for me, too. Sharing this birthday celebration with my peers helped softened the blow.

After an evening of non-stop reminiscing, drinking, and dancing, everyone was going out to the beach for a bonfire to continue the party into the wee hours of the morning. Ari and I had other things on our mind, and everyone wished us an enjoyable night.

As soon as Ari and I came home from the party, I immediately called Jennifer who was patiently waiting for the play by play details of the weekend. She knew almost everyone I was talking about, which made it so much fun to share my stories with her. We made plans for the following Saturday night to go out for dinner with our husbands. Tammy brought Prince home and all went well.

After having my typical Saturday morning of working out, breakfast, and a quick shower, Jennifer came over and we just chilled. As soon as she walked in, she went straight to my closet to try on any tops or pants I may want to get rid of.

"Hey Jen, I have a question. Do you have any regrets that you and Marv didn't have any children?"

"Are you kidding me? No way. You know how much I hate responsibility. Besides, between my brother and sister I have six nieces and nephews, and I send the kids gifts all the time," she answered honestly.

"Dori tell me something, who will take care of us when we are old and frail?" Jennifer asked, while we were enjoying a comfortable silence.

"Our husbands, silly." I said.

"But what if?" She asked.

"Don't go there, Jen; nothing is going to happen. We'll just have to take care of each other." I said.

Later that night, we met our new best friends for dinner. Afterwards, I noticed that Marv was a little sad. Jennifer had told me that his grandmother had passed away at the age of ninety-seven. She was a wonderful woman, and was the glue that held his family together. Marv was her favorite grandson and everyone knew it.

House of Mourning

His family was sitting *Shiva* (house of mourning) at his aunt's house. They ordered a deli tray from Ari, who personally delivered it and brought along a gift of dessert as well. Ari and I didn't attend, but Jennifer called while she was there to thank us for the food. While we were talking, Marv's aunt got on the phone.

"Dori honey, my mother really loved you and so do I. You will always be my niece," she said warmly.

"Thank you so much, Auntie Fannie. I'm so touched and I will always love you, too," I said feeling *farclempt (choked up)* by her loving words. I felt a few tears dribble down my cheek.

"What an amazing situation we have," Jennifer said as she took the phone back from her.

"I know. We even share the same *machetunim* (in-laws). We are surrounded by so much love, peace and harmony. Aren't you amazed how all this turned out? Who knew? " I asked.

"Yea, yea, yea," she added, having exhausted her emotions. "But, Dori I'm her niece now, so there," she said, and we both laughed.

"Love you."

"Love you, too," she responded as we hung up the phone.

Thanksgiving was approaching, as was my big fiftieth birthday. Turning fifty was a milestone in my life. However, I have never felt better and according to Ari, this is the best I have ever looked. My layers of protection have vanished, and I finally have true acceptance of who I am. This is a much easier way of life rather than trying to block out or cover up my imperfections.

The real radiance comes from within. I'm finally free to be my true self, not just as an adult, but also as a woman, a wife, and now an author. This is one of my life's greatest gifts that I worked very hard to achieve.

"Baby, I have been thinking about what I want to do for my big five-oh." I told Ari over dinner.

"What's that honey?" He asked.

"I really don't want any fuss. I just want to go out of town, just you and me." I said.

"We can do anything you want," Ari lovingly responded. A few days later I booked a week in Puerto Vallarta. We left two days later, right after Thanksgiving. Ari and I celebrated my birthday on the beach, having a candlelight dinner under the moon and the stars, while enjoying our breathtaking life.

CHAPTER EIGHTEEN

"I Hear a Symphony"

The Supremes

When we returned home, Ari began a long search for just the right location for our fourth deli in the heart of Detroit.

"Baby, don't you think three stores are enough?" I asked.

"Yes, but I love the challenge of turning S**t into gold. I love to win in the game of life. But if I don't win, at least I played the game to the best of my ability," he expressed honestly from his heart.

"I want my husband to be well and healthy. And no matter how hard you try, the delis can't run successfully without you. Aren't you spreading yourself too thin? We don't need anymore stores."

"It's not a matter of need. If I have you by my side and have your support, that's enough for me."

"I know this is important to you, especially when everyone else lost faith in you. I love you so much, Husband. You have my support and always will," I said.

There had been a lot of new construction going on in the downtown center area including a skating rink, which is a take-off on Rockefeller Center in New York. There are fabulous restaurants, fancy jazz clubs, and thriving new businesses; a transformation exciting to see. The purchase of our new store was being handled by me, which I just loved doing. It also kept my finger on the pulse of the industry. We planned to close on the new location early next year.

Ari and I had the annual Chanukah party for the family at our house this year. We had the traditional potato *latkes* (pancakes) and everyone exchanged very special and loving gifts. Zachary had bought me a very touching card along with a beautiful candle, and Renee gave me the biggest surprise of all. She baked a birthday cake for both Holly and me because our birthdays are a day apart.

She also hand made a sexy, black cocktail dress just for me. I really loved it and after a little coaxing from the family I tried it on and to my astonishment, it fit perfectly.

"Come on, let's see you!" Ari called out.

As I paused at the entry of our living room where everyone was waiting, I took a deep breath and stepped in, and everyone clapped and whistled at the dress. Renee was jumping up and down feeling so proud of her accomplishment. She also brought us one other surprise, a small longhaired white kitten. We named her Madison. Ari fell in love with her, too, even though he never wanted another cat since Samantha. I was touched by Renee's warmth and generosity. I truly felt she once again was back in our lives.

The following Sunday, Ari and I went downstairs and worked out. Afterwards, we took a sauna and showered, absorbing all the good feelings from exercising. Six o'clock rolled around and we needed to decide where we were going for dinner. I walked into the bedroom and Ari looked amazing as he lay in bed wearing only his black bikini underwear. He smiled as I cuddled in his arms. I was famished and only thinking about eating dinner, not anything else.

"How about I call for Chinese carry out?" I asked him. He didn't say a word.

"I know, let's go to the Asian Grill and we'll share our favorite crispy duck. How does that sound to you?" I suggested.

After a long pause of silence, he whispered in my ear, "Get ready, you have five minutes."

Quickly, I threw on my sexy black cat suit with "the Girl's" front and center and I slipped into my black stilettos. I planned on keeping his flame simmering during dinner.

We sat together in a cozy booth, while having a delicious dinner. Out of nowhere he said, "You have what every woman wants."

"I do? What's that, Honey?" I asked with surprise.

"You have long blonde hair, a small waist, nice hips, shapely long legs, a great smile and an ass to die for."

"Thank you so much, Honey, but what about my mind and personality?"

We both cracked up and hugged each other tightly. My husband rushed through his dinner and couldn't seem to get out of there fast enough. We quickly said goodbye to some people we knew as we rushed by them. I smiled to myself and thought how lucky I was to have a husband who loves me and wants me this much.

"You've Given Me a True Love."

When we walked into the house, Ari walked straight into the bedroom and got into bed and I followed him.

"Honey, do you want anything?" I asked slipping off my shoes.

"You!" he said firmly, as I lit the candelabra and fell right into bed. Our lovemaking began with great intensity. Once our eyes met, our hands began to roam over each other's bodies. Ari's hands found and caressed every erogenous zone on my body. My burning desire for him was hungrier than I ever thought possible. My very being was screaming, while at the same time my body was throbbing all over. No words were exchanged nor needed to be.

His organ became harder with each touch and my body burned while dripping with love for Ari. As I looked deep and hard into the windows of his soul, my breath became more rapid, my moaning was intense, until I could no longer restrain myself. He entered me slowly and with a piercing scream of ecstasy and passion, we were feverishly out of our minds climaxing while becoming one.

As we lay in the afterglow of our love, Ari looked into the windows of my soul and held my face inside his warm tender hands.

"Shh, don't talk. Touching you and looking into your beautiful eyes is my way of talking," he said softly.

"You are so beautiful," he whispered. I melted deeper into his arms, as we bathed in the moisture of our lovemaking.

To me, life really did begin at forty. But each day is brand new. By taking charge and learning that I had to be the one to change, my life turned around and it gets better every day. Everything in my life used to be temporary. However, Ari held the key that unlocked the depth of my insecurities. With his endless love and devotion, I now have permanence, enabling me to trust again and to love him unconditionally. I'm no longer a people-pleaser. Finally in the truest sense of the word, I know who I am. I also know that it was *bashert* (fated) that Ari and I would meet.

"Do you remember honey, that Friday in the fall of 1995, the night we met, and how we both owned our own real estate company and you told me you had a staff of one?" He asked as we lay in bed.

"Yeah, and you told me that you had a staff of one, too," I replied.

"Yeah, well guess what? One plus one equals perfect. I love you, Woman," he said in his masculine sexy voice.

"I love you more!" I said.

"I doubt it." Ari assured me and we embraced.

My life has been an extreme make-over on the slow payment plan. Though there were no facelifts or plastic surgeries, there had been a life lift. All of my nips and tucks were accomplished by the bumps and bruises caused by the bad choices I made and the effects from others as well. I refused to let the scars of life break my spirit and I never will.

"Then Suddenly, I Hear a Symphony."

Turning fifty years old can be a midlife crisis or a celebration. I chose to celebrate; I have never felt so young or more alive as I do today. The moment of truth came when I learned to take charge of my own life and with a little help I got through the tough stuff. I truly believe G-d still watches over me and I thank Him daily. He has been there for me because I have continued to work on myself. Now I walk with a meaningful smile along with the confidence that experience and maturity brings. My past is finally where it belongs, in the past.

I still wear many hats at one time, but this time they are hats I choose to wear, and they fit perfectly. It is Ari's and my goal to celebrate fifty years together, even though we will be nearly one hundred years old. As long as we eat right, practice yoga, and, most of all, he continues to chase me around the house; we will make it. We're married seven years now and he constantly says, "You ain't seen nothin' yet!"

Now, in my dream, instead of holding the hands of two young girls (who I believe were Lori and I) and singing "Fly Me to the Moon", I'm holding the hand of the man I love, and together we are "Singing the Song of Life."

The Beginning